SUCCESSFUL ENGLISH

BOOK 2

JUDY CONLAN
AMANDA FORD
ELIZABETH HAYWOOD
MARIE HENLEY
HEATHER MCINTOSH

OXFORD
UNIVERSITY PRESS

OXFORD
UNIVERSITY PRESS

253 Normanby Road, South Melbourne, Victoria 3205, Australia

Oxford University Press is a department of the University of Oxford. It furthers the University's objective of excellence in research, scholarship, and education by publishing worldwide in

Oxford New York

Auckland Cape Town Dar es Salaam Hong Kong Karachi Kuala Lumpur Madrid Melbourne Mexico City Nairobi New Delhi Shanghai Taipei Toronto

With offices in

Argentina Austria Brazil Chile Czech Republic France Greece Guatemala Hungary Italy Japan Poland Portugal Singapore South Korea Switzerland Thailand Turkey Ukraine Vietnam

First published 2006

National Library of Australia
Cataloguing-in-Publication data:
Successful English.

For year 8 secondary students.

ISBN 978 0 19 555538 7. ISBN 978 0 19 555535 6.
ISBN 0 19 555538 4 (bk 2: Teacher's bk). ISBN 0 19 555535 X.

1. English language—Texbooks. 2. English language—Problems, exercises, etc.—Textbooks. I. Ford, Amanda, 1948- .

372.6

Typeset by J&M Typesetting

Printed in Hong Kong by Sheck Wah Tong Printing Press Ltd

CONTENTS

PREFACE

Successful English Student's Book 2 will help students in the second year of secondary school to improve all aspects of their English. The book has been designed with flexibility in mind, and is divided into four sections: Grammar, Spelling, Comprehension and Writing.

GRAMMAR

This section is designed to help students improve their grammar and writing skills. Each unit begins with a brief yet clear explanation of a point of grammar, followed by a range of activities. All the basics of grammar are covered, and activities are fun and relevant, allowing students to practise grammar skills in context. Within each unit there is a range of activity types catering to a variety of learning styles. The exercises are graded within each unit and so will satisfy students of different abilities.

SPELLING

This section will help students improve their spelling and build their vocabulary. Each full-page unit begins with a panel of words followed by a range of activities. Unit topics are engaging and require students to use the words in context.

COMPREHENSION

This section is designed to help students improve their reading comprehension skills. Each double-page unit presents a text followed by a range of questions. A wide range of text types is presented, including fiction extracts, news and magazine articles, instructions, letters, poems and advertisements. Passages are interesting and engaging, and can be used as the basis for further class activities.

WRITING

This section will help students develop their writing skills. Each double-page unit examines a different technique or genre of writing and presents examples followed by a range of questions. A wide range of fiction and non-fiction text types is covered, including informative, narrative, descriptive, instructive and persuasive. The exercises include creative activities and real-life tasks that require students to develop specific writing skills.

Each section of *Successful English* can be worked through sequentially, used in conjunction with other sections, or individual units can be selected to support a particular class or student. The units are ideal for homework exercises or classroom use.

TEACHER'S BOOK

Successful English Teacher's Book 2 provides answers to all of the units in the Student's Book. Where a range of responses is possible, no answer is provided. The *Writing* section of the Teacher's Book contains a series of criteria checklists appropriate to each activity (as a range of responses is possible in the writing activities), which teachers can use as a guide to assessing the development and capabilities of their students.

ACKNOWLEDGMENTS

The authors and publisher wish to thank the following copyright holders for granting permission to reproduce their material.

ACP Publishing for 'Young Doctors' from *Dolly* magazine, August, 2001; *The Age* and Claire Miller for 'First the cattle, now for the brumbies', *The Age*, 19/6/05; Department of Education, Science and Training for 'Stunt Performer' from *Job Guide 2001*; Harcourt Education for the extract from *Introduced Plants and Animals* by Greg Pyers, Heinemann Library, 2001; The Herald & Weekly Times for 'Hooning future foretold' by Susie O'Brien, *Herald Sun*, 3/6/05, 'Hop into Hanoi' by Alan Hill, *Herald Sun*, 7/11/01, 'Old man's many moods' by Richard Cornish, *Herald Sun*, 3/8/01; David Higham Associates for the extract from *Boy* by Roald Dahl, published by Jonathan Cape Ltd & Penguin Books Ltd; Dr Richard Lawrence, Ballarat Veterinary Practice for 'Going down like lead', *Herald Sun*, 28/7/01; Lonely Planet Publications for 'Hawaiian Monk Seal' from *Hawaii 5th edition*, Lonely Planet Books, 2000; Lothian Books for the extract from *Scam* by Jenny Pausacker, Lothian Books, 2001; Kim Luke for 'Seascape'; Penguin Group (Australia) for the extract from *The Silver Fox* by Rosemary Hayes, Puffin Books, 1987; Penguin Group (New Zealand) for 'Chocolate' from *The Fat Man* by Maurice Gee, Penguin Books (NZ), 1994.

The authors and publisher would also like to acknowledge these sources:

Manches & Co. Solicitors and the Estate of J.R.R. Tolkien for 'Far Over the Misty Mountains' from *The Hobbit* by J.R.R. Tolkien. Copyright © J.R.R. Tolkien 1937; Wayland Publishers Ltd for 'The Conquistadors' from *Exploration in History* by Sheila Robertson, first published in 1984.

Every effort has been made to trace the original source of copyright material contained in this book. The publisher would be pleased to hear from copyright holders to rectify any errors or omissions.

Grammar

HEATHER MCINTOSH

This section introduces the essential rules of grammar and word usage. Topics are introduced with a concise definition and clear examples, using a minimum of linguistic terminology. The activities are designed to be fun and engaging, and allow grammar skills to be practised in context. Each of the thirty-four units is a stand-alone worksheet, and they can be worked through sequentially or used in any order.

Grammar Grammar Grammar

GRAMMAR UNIT 1 PARTS OF SPEECH (REVISION)

1 Let's jog your memory.

a How many parts of speech are there? ________________

b What is a conjunction? ________________

c What part of speech is used to show strong emotion or attitude? ________________

d What do adjectives describe? ________________

e List five proper nouns. ________________

f What job does a noun perform? ________________

____

g Give five examples of a verb. ________________

h Prepositions link nouns or pronouns with other words. Give five examples of a preposition. ________________

i What do adverbs do? ________________

j What part of speech can replace a noun? ________________

k How many articles are there? List them. ________________

2 What part of speech are the following words?

a lazy ________ **f** try ________

b lazily ________ **g** but ________

c hazel ________ **h** quickly ________

d simple ________ **i** quick ________

e the ________ **j** it ________

3 Place appropriate adverbs in the spaces provided.

a The doctor ________ called for an ambulance.

b Alana spied a centipede ________ inching its way across the toilet floor.

c We watched in awe as the hot-air balloon ________ came down to land.

d ________ the thief tiptoed across the marble floor.

e Sarah ________ posed for the photographer. She loved all the attention!

4 Circle all the nouns in this list.

irony, prudent, convoy, their, shipwrecked, nice, nicely, supremacy, quit, gestation, across, sing, vendetta, heavy, willow, fossil, catty, disparity, horrendous, annoying, fad, burped, falcon, goggles, hover, sparse, inquest, inward, in, Petri dish, status, trousers, mayonnaise, flute, celestial, invade, dragster, because, faith, arachnophobia, dromedary, drought, dignity, invasion, motherboard, talkative, knave, badly, backpack

5 Write a description of a train trip in 15–20 lines. Include a minimum of 10 adjectives, 20 nouns, 10 verbs, 5 prepositions, 5 conjunctions and 3 interjections in your description.

GRAMMAR UNIT 2 NOUNS (REVISION)

GRAMMAR

1 Answer the following questions.

a What is a concrete noun? ______

b Give five examples of an abstract noun. ______

c What sort of noun should always have a capital letter? ______

d Give ten examples of a common noun. ______

e Define a proper noun. ______

f What sort of noun is the word *army*? ______

2 Make the following nouns plural.

a beach ______

b woman ______

c seagull ______

d fraternity ______

e salmon ______

f tax ______

g calf ______

h lady ______

i mistake ______

j lunch ______

k foot ______

l child ______

3 Place appropriate proper nouns in the spaces provided.

a Our family is flying to ______ for the ______ holidays.

b ______ is the President of the United States.

c ______ is the capital of ______.

d My best friend, ______, lives in ______.

e ______ started arguing with ______, so he received an hour's detention.

4 These words are all nouns. Name the type of noun.

a bravery ______

b Stephanie ______

c tractor ______

d swarm ______

e Tasmania ______

f fleet ______

g starvation ______

h Ringo Starr ______

i earth ______

j fencing ______

k prosperity ______

l diligence ______

5 Write an imaginative composition about an escape. It could be from a zoo, prison, alien planet or terrible situation. What about an escape from responsibilities? Include the following in your story:

- lots of common nouns
- ten proper nouns
- ten abstract nouns
- ten concrete nouns
- five collective nouns

GRAMMAR UNIT 3 FIRST, SECOND AND THIRD PERSON

GRAMMAR

All forms of writing can be described as being written in the first, second or third person. This refers to the 'voice' of a piece of writing. A person is either doing the speaking (**first person**), being spoken to (**second person**) or being spoken about (**third person**).

Texts written in the first person use the personal pronouns *I* and *we*.

I attend Mass every Sunday. *I* go with my family and *we* always sit in the same pew.

Texts written in the second person use the personal pronoun *you*. This is both singular and plural.

You are going to regret *your* behaviour tonight. *You* have disgraced *your*selves.

Texts written in the third person use the personal pronouns *he, she, it* and *they.*

He decided to spoil *his* wife and book a holiday in Bali, where *they* could relax.

It is important that there is always agreement between verbs and pronouns.

I *am* running. **not** I *is* running. He *dances* well. **not** He *dance* well.

1 Rewrite the following text in the first person.

Trixie seriously regrets her decision to start ballet lessons. Her teacher is bossy, impatient and far too strict for her liking. She doesn't like the other students and feels as though she doesn't fit in. She thinks they are all significantly more talented than she is and laugh behind her back. She has been attending for a month, but it's unlikely that she'll continue for much longer.

2 This letter is a dreadful mixture of the first, second and third person. Decide in which person the letter should be written and rewrite it correctly.

Dear Mrs Tabernackle,

We is writing to complain about the quality of education you are offering our son.

They carefully investigated all local primary schools and they decided The Whippersnapper School for Boys was the best option for their son Pontius. The last few months, however, have made them doubt the correctness of their choice. Twelve times, over the past three months, Pontius have arrived home distraught and in tears because I felt my needs was not being met. On one occasion, Pontius explained, their teacher incorrectly admonished us for not sharing painting equipment. I am a bright and vivacious child who needs to be encouraged in my endeavours, but rather than enjoy my educational experience, I am constantly unhappy and frustrated.

You trust that this letter will result in an increase in Pontius' happiness. Otherwise you will have to consider withdrawing him from our institution.

Yours sincerely,

Mr and Mrs Pimpernel

GRAMMAR UNIT 4 POSSESSIVE PRONOUNS

Personal pronouns replace nouns that name people, animals or things. *me*, *he*, *she*, *it*, *they*, *us*

Possessive pronouns are personal pronouns that indicate ownership or possession.

First person: *my*, *mine*, *our*, *ours*

Second person: *you*, *yours*

Third person: *his*, *her*, *hers*, *its*, *their*, *theirs*

You should *never* use an apostrophe with possessive pronouns.

1 Complete these sentences with an appropriate possessive pronoun.

a 'That's our video!' shouted Ben. 'That's __________!'

b Penelope lost her ruler and had to use __________.

c Roy and Ray asked to borrow our mower while __________ was being fixed.

d The company liquidated __________ assets.

e Our budgie broke __________ wing when it tried to escape from __________ cage.

f Haylee bites ______ lips when _______ brother teases her in front of __________ friends.

2 Each of these sentences contains two errors. Rewrite the sentences correctly.

a 'Do you think Don's party will be as good as our?' Jill asked hers husband.

____

b Their not your slippers, Gerald. Your are in your room.

____

c The sparrow turned it's head towards the noise, flapped it's wings and flew away.

____

d The weary travellers were relieved to finally reach his destination and unpack our bags for the last time.

____

____

e Stephanie never files or cuts her nails. She says its a waste of hers precious time. She just bites them.

____

____

3 Underline the noun to which the possessive pronoun refers.

For example: Gina looked at Tim's shoes. 'Are they yours?' she asked.

a My mother wanted to know if the money was mine.

b The tiny octopus wound its tentacles around the spiky coral.

c Jeff was insanely jealous of Rob and Kelly's new computer. Theirs was far more powerful than his.

d 'Why isn't our house as nice as Fiona's?' whinged Madeleine. 'Ours is a dump.'

e The recession is getting worse. Its grip on consumer confidence is frightening.

GRAMMAR UNIT 5 PRESENT AND PAST PARTICIPLES

The **present** and **past participles** are non-finite verbs. They are verbs that **cannot stand alone**. They need an auxiliary verb to make sense.

The **present participle** always ends in *-ing* and indicates that an action is being carried out.

She is *dancing*. They are *playing*. It is *raining*.

The **past participle** often ends in *-ed* or *-en* but can take many forms. It indicates that an action occurred in the past.

The money had *gone*. They had *known*. Have you *looked*? It was *written*.

1 Circle the present participles and underline the auxiliary verbs in these sentences.

a He was being tortured.

b The baby is blowing bubbles.

c Buying bathers is always a trial.

d That noise is driving me mad.

e She had a sinking feeling.

2 Circle the past participles and underline the auxiliary verbs in these sentences.

a They were the chosen ones.

b Valerie knew she had drunk too much.

c I just couldn't remember where I'd hidden the key.

d We had sworn to tell the truth.

e I suspect that little experience has taught you a lesson.

3 Place an appropriate present participle in the space provided.

a Don't disturb your father. He is ____________.

b I think the Canadian is ____________ in lane 3.

c Leon was ____________ a tantrum when I arrived.

d We are ____________ about going away next weekend.

e The headmaster is ____________ my mother about my recent detentions.

f Mitchell is ____________, ____________ and ____________ with his mates.

4 Place an appropriate past participle in the space provided.

a The water was ____________ before we drank it.

b The poor man was ____________ senseless.

c Our frightened dog was ____________ down by two veterinary assistants.

d My twin sisters are always ____________ identical presents.

e I couldn't believe the pond had ____________ overnight.

f They were ____________, ____________ and ____________ before dawn.

5 Circle the auxiliary verbs in exercises 3 and 4.

GRAMMAR UNIT 6 TYPES OF ADJECTIVES

Adjectives qualify or modify nouns by describing things, such as size, shape, colour, number, taste, attitude, direction, age, weight and sound.

The *bright*, *shiny* car caught our attention.

The *whispering* brook flowed past the *ancient*, *proud* birches.

The *ferocious* wind blew the *tiny* boats further out into the *cruel*, *unforgiving* sea.

Note that when more than one adjective is used, a comma is used to separate all but the last adjective.

The small, quick, brown fox jumped over the dirty, stinking stile.

There are several different types of adjectives:

Proper adjectives are formed from proper nouns and usually need a capital letter.

an *Irish* legend

Descriptive adjectives describe the *quality* of something.

bitter end, *good* results, *tasty* lunch, *proud* parents

Quantitative adjectives indicate *how much*.

I need *some* help. There is *little* room.

Adjectives of number indicate the actual number of things being written about.

six books, *a hundred bucks*

1 Place an appropriate adjective in the space provided.

a The ____________ patient hopped up onto the bed as the doctor instructed.

b There's nothing worse than ____________ fish and chips.

c I could hardly see through the ____________ and ____________ light.

d Gregory tried to block out his ____________ nightmares from last night.

e Three ____________, ____________ elephants trundled past.

2 Place quantitative adjectives in the spaces provided.

a I don't like mashed potato ____________.

b There was an ____________ amount of money in the fund.

c I think I could do with ____________ respect around here.

d I'm sorry, Mrs Martin, but there has been ____________ improvement in your son's condition. It will be a ____________ while before we know ____________ more.

3 Place descriptive adjectives in the spaces provided.

a ____________ moth's wings

b the deer's ____________ eyes

c ____________ jeans

d ____________, ____________ giraffe

e my ____________ ambitions

f her ____________ behaviour

g ____________ dandruff

h ____________, ____________ ears

i our dad's ____________ past

j the mountain ____________, ____________

k a ____________ and ____________ letter

l ignoring a ____________, ____________ and ____________ vagrant

4 Put your understanding and appreciation of adjectives to use! Describe a meeting of two strangers on a dark night. Use adjectives to create atmosphere, tension and a really vivid picture in the reader's mind.

GRAMMAR UNIT 7 COMPARATIVE ADJECTIVES

Adjectives are often used to compare people and things. They can be used in three forms:
Positive: She is *brave*.
Comparative (comparing two things): She is *braver* than Sue.
Superlative (comparing three or more things): She is the *bravest* in the group.
To form the comparative, add *-r* or *-er* or use the word *more*.

great/greater eager/more eager

To form the superlative, add *-est* or use the word *most*.

great/greatest smelly/most smelly

Some adjectives are compared irregularly.

bad→worse→worst good→better→best little→less→least many→more→most

1 Underline the comparative adjectives in these sentences.

a That's the worst film I have ever seen.
b Cross the river where it is widest.
c Magpies are smaller than eagles.
d We found the most beautiful necklace for Olivia.
e From here, the pool is further than the gym.

2 Match each noun from the left column with a comparative adjective from the right column. Then write a sentence using the two words.

Nouns	Comparative adjectives	Sentences
donation	more aggressive	____________
Rottweiler	most generous	____________
insect	most stupid	____________
sheep	clever	____________
student	colder	____________
Melbourne	strangest	____________

3 Fill in the spaces in this table with comparative adjectives.

Positive	Comparative	Superlative
deep		deepest
fast	faster	
	stranger	strangest
	lonelier	
		silliest
pathetic	more pathetic	
		most destructive
inventive		
good		best
much	more	

GRAMMAR UNIT 8 ADVERBS

GRAMMAR

Adverbs are words that are added to a verb to give more information about that verb.

John runs *quickly*. Katie sings *beautifully*. Terry drives *dangerously*.

Adverbs can also give more information about adjectives or other adverbs.

The *very* slow car caused a traffic jam. He runs *extremely* quickly.

Adverbs answer questions about the action of the verb, such as *how?*, *when?* or *where?*

She opened the window *quietly*. (tells *how* she opened the window)

Robert jumped the fence *immediately*. (tells *when* he jumped the fence)

Frances looked for her necklace *everywhere*. (tells *where* she looked)

Most adverbs are formed by adding *-ly* to the adjective.

slow/slowly silent/silently modest/modestly

Adverbs may be **comparative**, that is, they indicate the **degree** of the action.

The army fought *bravely*. (positive)

The army fought *more bravely*. (comparative)

The army fought *most bravely*. (superlative)

Adverbs are used to make sentences more precise and interesting.

1 Turn the following adjectives into adverbs.

a cool ______________ **f** calm ______________
b sick ______________ **g** happy ______________
c strange ______________ **h** remote ______________
d frightening ______________ **i** inhospitable ______________
e sensible ______________ **j** malodorous ______________

2 Complete these sentences with an appropriate adverb. Then underline the word that each adverb is modifying.

a The car spun out of control but ____________ missed hitting anything.
b ____________ I locked myself out of the house.
c George was given a bravery award because he behaved so ____________.
d The photographer ____________ observed the birds fly ____________ past.
e We ____________ realised we'd been burgled.
f Disposing of nuclear waste is an ____________ serious problem.

3 Choose an adverb from this list to fill in each space.

definitely silently noisily loudly nervously tightly thickly happily closely

The riverbank had been quiet for weeks: no children had ridden past ____________, no boats had zoomed ____________ past, and no other campers had ____________ arrived to set up camp. Mike and Julie liked to go to faraway places to holiday, but now they were starting to think ____________ that this was a strange place. One day they saw a grey scum floating ____________ on the water. The next day a swan appeared ____________. Mike looked ____________ at it and found a note tied ____________ around its neck. This place was ____________ weird.

GRAMMAR UNIT 9 ADVERBS AND ADJECTIVES

You already know how to use adverbs and adjectives, but it is easy to confuse them.

Adjectives describe nouns and pronouns by providing extra information about things, such as colour, size, amount, taste, weight, age and direction. They usually precede a noun or follow a verb.

This is a *steep* driveway. The driveway is *steep*. I am a *fast* runner. I can run *fast*.

Adverbs usually end in *-ly* and answer the when/where/how questions about verbs, adjectives and other adverbs.

They *gently* rocked. It *slowly* burnt. We kissed *passionately*. He will arrive *soon*.
She is *quite* pretty. It jolted *suddenly*. They very *quickly* realised. We were *really* pleased.

Make sure you do not accidentally use an **adjective** instead of an **adverb**.

Incorrect: Debbie was *real* shocked. (*Real* is an adjective. Adjectives do *not* describe verbs.)
Correct: Debbie was *really* shocked. (*Really* is an adverb. Adverbs *do* describe verbs.)

1 For each word, identify the part of speech.

a We ____ drank ____ quickly. ____

b You ____ are ____ the ____ tallest. ____

c The ____ shops ____ are ____ busier ____ on ____ Saturday. ____

d The ____ submarine ____ slowly ____ submerged. ____

e They ____ are ____ easily ____ mistaken. ____

2 Provide more information about these verbs by supplying an adverb.

a He limps ____________.
b You write ____________.
c The children play ____________.
d Don't scream so ____________.
e The soldiers marched ____________.
f Tracy ____________ sobbed.
g I was ____________ teased.
h The alarm was ____________ raised.
i Please write more ____________.
j Ian argued ____________.
k ____________ justifying his comment.
l ____________ displayed on the mantelpiece.

3 Circle the correct word in the following sentences.

a She plays the violin well/good.
b He's a well/good sport.
c I'm real/really tired.
d Please close the door quietly/quiet.
e Run to the shops quick/quickly.
f The truck slow/slowly passed.
g I hate being stuck in the slow/slowly lane.
h Why do you eat so slow/slowly?
i He set the table nicely/nice.
j Thank your grandmother nicely/nice.
k Lachlan laughed loud/loudly.
l Laughing loudly/loud, Lachlan leered.

GRAMMAR UNIT 10 COMMAS

GRAMMAR

Here are some examples to remind you about how to use commas.

Mark, Jade's oldest brother, gave us a lift.	Tired but elated, we locked the door and left.
Brian, feed the cat please.	The concert being over, the lights came on.
It was a long, tiring, dusty ride.	Sanjay yelled, but we remained silent.
New York, my favourite city, is beautiful in autumn.	When the clock struck one, the mouse ran down.
We bought green, yellow, red and blue streamers.	Alex said, 'Please forgive me.'

1 Place commas in the correct places in the following sentences.

a Penny purchased the printer scanner monitor and keyboard using her credit card.
b The vicious tornado swept over Florida Alabama Georgia and South Carolina.
c Cromwell's eyes though set very wide apart were small and beady.
d With so much going on she had not had time she told herself to think of Edmund.
e After a glance at the boy's stricken face Uncle Tom explained he was joking.
f 'I fear' Portia said smoothly 'there will be no compensation.'
g He had not like James attended a good school and therefore felt disadvantaged.

2 Mission: Impossible! Your task, should you choose to accept it, is to place thirty-three commas in their correct places in the following text. (You can tick off the commas as you go.)

, ,

Ronan was petrified he'd be caught. They'd thought through the plan six seven eight maybe even nine times but there were still enormous risks. What if Josie had panicked told Frank Stevie or Jimmy called the cops or warned the bank? Ronan just didn't know what to expect when he opened that vent. He carried his Colt 45 an old Browning a switchblade and a stun grenade but he was still nervous. He thought about Fifi and his three little girls Jasmine Lily and Rose. What would they do without him? Fifi would kill him if she knew what he was up to. The girls however would be proud. Oh! His sweet little girls! He loved Jazzy Lil and Ro with a passion. They'd understand. They'd know he was doing it for them. They'd know that the late nights missed holidays sudden departures and forgotten birthdays were all for a reason. He didn't like what he was doing but it was necessary. Ronan tried to concentrate on the job ahead of him. He just couldn't afford to become distracted lose focus or forget the intricate details of the plan. He looked at his watch. There wasn't much time left. Doors two four six and nine had to be blown in thirteen minutes. Ronan picked up his trusty old rucksack his tool kit the ropes and carabineers and shook his head clear. Prior preparation and planning he thought is everything. There is of course the possibility that misfortune could intervene ruin all plans and destroy the mission. But it wasn't likely. Not with him Ronan Del Guado on the job. Ronan took one last look around the dusty room patted his two holsters kissed his crucifix and bent down to prise open the airconditioning vent. He just never saw the screaming spinning bullet that knocked him backwards …

GRAMMAR UNIT 11 COLONS (:)

A **colon** is a punctuation mark used to join two parts of a sentence. The colon indicates that the information that follows is an explanation or elaboration of what precedes it.

> The situation is clear: if you fail to study sufficiently, you will not pass the final examination.

Here the colon is used to explain *why* the situation is clear. See how the information that follows the colon *explains* the statement that precedes the colon. The words that follow a colon may or may not form a complete sentence. In some cases it may be only one word.

Colons are also used to introduce lists.

> Items stolen from my purse included: two credit cards, a driver's licence, a library card, three video cards and cash.

Colons are also used to introduce a quotation or definition.

> My favourite line from *Romeo and Juliet*: 'they have made worms' meat of me'.

Grammatically speaking, a colon is not as strong as a full stop. It creates a pause shorter than a full stop but longer than a comma.

1 Insert colons into the following sentences to make them grammatically correct.

- **a** It's not safe out there three murderers, four terrorists and a score of petty criminals are on the loose.
- **b** The doctor had no choice the leg had to come off.
- **c** It's simple you stay or you go.
- **d** Who said 'Out damned spot! Out, I say'?
- **e** Harry was most pleased with his purchases new shoes, jeans, a T-shirt and a cap.
- **f** By Friday, Ross was thrilled with his efforts he'd arrived early to work every day.
- **g** Halitosis the proper word for bad breath.
- **h** Please don't buy any more peanuts I'm allergic to them.
- **i** Vadim was vexed was the word 'vacuum' a verb or a noun?
- **j** Dian lived by only one proverb he that burns most shines most.

2 Complete these sentences. Remember that the information that follows a colon is a list, definition, quotation or an explanation of the first part of the sentence.

- **a** These are the foods I hate:
- **b** Adjective:
- **c** David is obsessed with a number of things:
- **d** There are lots of reasons why I said no:
- **e** She swung around and looked at me in horror:
- **f** Best line from a film:

3 See if you can write six sentences containing a colon.

4 Imagine that you come home from school one day and your dad wants to know what you have learnt. You tell him that you learnt all about colons.
He is amazed. He wants it all explained. Write your explanation of what a colon is and when it is used, and provide your dad with some examples.

GRAMMAR UNIT 12 SEMI-COLONS (;)

GRAMMAR

Despite its name, the semi-colon is not simply half a colon: it has a job of its own. A **semi-colon** is used to link two complete sentences that are closely related. This allows for the joining of ideas on the same subject.

It was a long, exhausting game; all players performed their best.

Semi-colons are also used to separate long, complicated lists. This allows for a slightly longer pause than that provided by a comma.

There was a dreadful number of injuries by half-time: Lucas pulled a hamstring; Marco's nose was broken; Mohammad twisted his ankle; Tony hurt his back; and three players came down with heat-stroke.

1 Insert semi-colons into the following sentences to make them grammatically correct.

a I really had forgotten how awful the house was: water dripped through mouldy ceilings floorboards creaked and squeaked ominously no door shut properly there were windows missing and the whole place stank of mice.

b The team leader was adamant about what was necessary to win: ferocious speed tireless strength well-timed coordination gutsy determination a fierce commitment to domination and a touch of foul play.

c Of course Robert could guess what would happen next he knew his girlfriend all too well.

d It was the best of times it was the worst of times.

e Hamlet had difficulty understanding Horatio's words how could his dear, dead father have been seen again?

f My best friend had thought of everything: wooden stakes hammer nails a bag of dry but stinking hay her mother's summer hat from last season, which she knew wouldn't be missed a flour bag old sneakers with huge holes in them and she'd even remembered to bring that dusty, dirty old jumper of her brother's. What a scarecrow we would make!

g Cohen felt frustrated by mystery novels he could never guess the endings. He preferred fantasy novels that actually let you choose what happened next recently published science fiction (not that old stuff) skimming through the Guinness Book of Records books about cricket and those American stories that are a bit like Harry Potter.

2 Place eight semi-colons into the following text. Cross off the semi-colons as you use them. ; ; ; ; ; ; ; ;

We had a brilliant holiday: it was hot it never rained the mosquitoes stayed away the campsite was excellent and we had plenty to do. Everyone was pleased with the two weeks away. Nicholas made new friends Jemima acquired a suntan Vedran learnt to surf and I enjoyed just chilling out. We'll definitely go away together again I've already booked the campsite for next Easter!

GRAMMAR UNIT 13 BRACKETS

Brackets are used to show extra information or an afterthought that has been added to a sentence.

Dylan and Joshua (Jon's brothers) stayed over last night.

No punctuation mark is necessary unless the information inside the brackets is an entire sentence.

Please feed the cat. (The food is in the fridge.)

Note that if the bracketed information is removed, the sentence should still make sense.

My grandparents (who are usually grumpy) made a special effort for my birthday.

Brackets are also known as **parentheses**.

1 **Place brackets in the correct places in the following sentences.**

- **a** We think well, I think, and your father agrees that you should be home by eleven.
- **b** I've just crashed my car! Actually it's my father's car!
- **c** A mistake was made only a tiny one and I was blamed.
- **d** The quarrel between my aunts started fifteen years ago is destroying our family.
- **e** Simone, Seth, Sammy and Steven but not Sigourney stayed until closing time.
- **f** The man in the blue Fiat the one I believe is responsible for this accident refused to give his name and address.
- **g** Place the thick wire blue on top of the thin wire green then twist the long wire brown onto the small ring labelled ring 1. Do not, under any circumstances, place the short wire purple into the largest ring labelled ring 3 as this will cause the primary piston silver to malfunction. The remaining wires yellow, black and white should be fitted to the remaining ring labelled ring 2.

2 **The writers of these notes did not know how to use brackets. Rewrite them, using brackets accurately.**

Mum and (Dad, if you're home),

I am sorry about the mess in the living room. Or should I call it (the disaster area?) Paul and I had a few people well, (maybe more than just a few over last night) and we haven't had a chance to clean. Paul did try but not very hard (to get rid of some of the bottles), but then he had to go to work. Mr Patel rang (late last night and asked him to do an extra shift).

Hope you enjoyed your weekend away. (How <u>are</u> Harvey and Nancy)?

Love Em xxx

Dear Amy,

Your mum I assume it was your mum rang the school and asked for work to be sent home. There is no homework (for Geography) miracle of miracles, but Mr Fisher set stacks of questions how unusual to be done by Friday for History. Old Doddy sorry, (<u>Mr</u> Dodds) wants the maths done by Monday. (Personally, I wouldn't stress about it;) he'll forget he even set it.

Sorry you are still sick. Everyone (except Ryan,) who's an idiot says hello.

Julie xxx

GRAMMAR UNIT 14 DASHES (—)

A **dash** (—) is used to emphasise additional information within a sentence.

He is a carpenter—a very successful and wealthy carpenter.

Dashes are often used in pairs. This provides greater emphasis than brackets or commas.

The advantages of selling—getting rid of unwanted stock and making a huge profit—far outweighed the disadvantages.

(Notice how the sentence still makes sense if you take out the information inside the dashes.)

Dashes can also be used to highlight a word or phrase at the end of a sentence. This indicates a pause and creates a special effect.

I'd be happy to be stuck on a desert island with anyone in the world—except you!

Not everyone loves Madonna—do you?

Dashes may be used non-punctuationally to replace missing letters or a whole word. (This is useful if you need to use a swear word but are not allowed!)

'D— you all!'

1 Where could you place a dash—or dashes—in the following sentences?

- **a** Dave walked into his newly painted room and nearly passed out in shock it was bright pink!
- **b** She wore a completely outrageous dress outrageous in the extreme.
- **c** Displaying the flag something that New Yorkers tend to do less than other Americans has become an important sign of defiance.
- **d** After we dragged ourselves over the steep rise, we saw something that made us despair another mountain.
- **e** Greg had everything in his life that he could ever want except hair.
- **f** After marking most of the essays 175 out of a total of 203 Mrs Di Marco realised that none of her students understood anything about the Russian Revolution.
- **g** Stevie is a difficult child a very confused, unhappy and immature child.
- **h** The city's leaders and its huge tourist industry must hope that this disaster does not keep tourists away forever.
- **i** Only three people were chosen for a second interview us!
- **j** Everything they needed balls, bats, stumps and pads were locked up in the equipment cupboard, but the coach had lost the keys.

2 Place a tick against the sentences that are grammatically correct.

- **a** Rupert enjoyed everything his wife cooked—except the curried kangaroo.
- **b** Liquid paper is very—useful.
- **c** I have only one person to blame—myself.
- **d** Gregory Deck a vicar—objected to the proposal—on moral grounds.
- **e** Keith Wong—a solicitor—objected to the proposal on legal grounds.

3 Now you can start to use dashes in your own writing. Write a tiny story about a tiny man and see if you can use at least ten dashes. (Don't make the dashes too tiny!)

GRAMMAR

GRAMMAR UNIT 15 HYPHENS (-)

A **hyphen** may look like a dash but beware: they are quite different!

A hyphen (-) is shorter than a dash—about half the length—and is used in a completely different way.

A **link hyphen** is used to join whole words or elements of words into longer words. These longer words are called *compounds*.

Anglo-Saxon ninety-nine runner-up open-air restaurant
non-French speakers happy-go-lucky

It is also used to join some prefixes and suffixes with a stem word to form a compound.

ex-President non-stick pre-empt Pre-Raphaelite cabbage-like

A **break hyphen** is used to indicate the division of a word at the end of a line, especially in newspapers, magazines and novels.

The famous Australian spread, Vege-
mite, was invented by a Melbourne man in 1923.

In handwritten and typed texts, it is normal to *avoid* breaking words in this way.

1 Here is a jumble of prefixes, suffixes and stem words. Use hyphens to match them up and form compounds. (You should be able to come up with ten compounds.)

infra step five event flight pre red jointed mother ex
pack giddy president fifty in up double student vice non

______ ______ ______ ______

______ ______ ______ ______

______ ______ ______ ______

2 Look at this text carefully and circle all the hyphens.

Most people consider the Brooke-Taylor expedition a success. Tom Brooke—a very ill man—and his long-standing friend, Bill Taylor, spent sixty-six days crossing the Musorian Plains—on foot. Many people before them—including the Flynn twins—had crossed the treacherous Plains before but not without some form of high-tech transport. Apparently, the two men had always wanted to walk across the ice-bound plains in south-east Inzerbaijan but high-ranking officials in the Inzerbaijani government had criticised the high-risk expedition and refused to lend their co-operation to what they labelled 'a ridiculous, half-baked idea'. It is report-ed that Brooke—encouraged by his wife—had a heart-to-heart with his doctor about the risks involved, re-routed the planned walk and wrote his will. The two friends stepped off an ice-breaker in early May and arrived at the far-western cor-ner of the Musorian Plains sixty-six days later. Brooke and Taylor admitted the trek had been difficult—Brooke developed pneumonia and Taylor discovered he was flat-footed—but believed their deep-seated faith in their abilities had got them through.

3 What do you think it means when someone says they are:

desk-bound? ______

ill-starred? ______

GRAMMAR UNIT 16

LINK HYPHENS

GRAMMAR

Unfortunately, the use of the link hyphen has always been unpredictable and it is often difficult to guess whether or not it should be used. The best thing to do is simply try to learn the most common compounds. If you are ever in doubt, consult a dictionary.

The following is a *very limited* list of common compounds:

non-alcoholic	ex-directory	infra-red	self-abuse	non-compliance
ex-libris	straight-laced	self-adhesive	non-essential	ex-serviceman
self-addressed	non-fattening	post-date	self-centred	non-fiction
anti-aircraft	post-haste	self-confidence	non-profit-making	anti-inflammatory
post-mortem	self-control	non-smoker	anti-nuclear	post-natal
self-defence	post-war	self-help	mother-in-law	pre-arrange
vice-president	pre-Christian	re-elect	two-thirds	clear-cut
pre-cook	re-enter	two-faced	well-known	pre-cut
re-evaluate	two-handed	red-hot	pre-empt	ready-made

1 Choose ten of the compounds listed above. Use each compound in a sentence, demonstrating that you understand what that compound means.

2 The above list gives you some idea of how many compounds there are. How many more can you think of? Write a list of as many compounds as you can. (Make sure each compound contains a link hyphen.)

3 Form compounds by adding a hyphen and a prefix, suffix or another word to the following words.

a father ____________	**l** war ____________
b war ____________	**m** red ____________
c confident ____________	**n** mortem ____________
d kart ____________	**o** play ____________
e independent ____________	**p** pistol ____________
f retired ____________	**q** go ____________
g iron ____________	**r** indulge ____________
h fortune ____________	**s** level ____________
i swimmer ____________	**t** out ____________
j saddle ____________	**u** best ____________
k Band ____________	**v** thought ____________

GRAMMAR

GRAMMAR UNIT 17 APOSTROPHES (REVISION)

Apostrophes have two functions:
They show possession or ownership.

Jo's plan — the girls' netball team — Isaac's Porsche

They form contractions by shortening words.

I can't go — you shouldn't — it's a problem

1 Insert apostrophes in the underlined words

a	whove	**g**	Peters nose	**m**	Ill
b	Im	**h**	youll be sorry	**n**	dont
c	whos coming?	**i**	theyd better hurry	**o**	some mens clubs
d	whats down the well?	**j**	hell	**p**	the Stevens house
e	well	**k**	hells an evil place	**q**	enquirys success
f	hadnt	**l**	a childs mind	**r**	Decembers elections

2 Sometimes even teachers get things wrong! Rewrite these reports ensuring you correct all the mistakes made with apostrophes.

Omars exam result's were impressive this term. Its clear hes been working hard. Omars' grasp of calculus has improved and his newfound understanding of differ-ential equation's will assist him consider-ably in the final exams. Im very happy with Omars contribution's in class and his homework is always of a high standard. Its a pleasure to have him in my class!	*Once again, its a joy for me to write Sarah's report. Shes such a lovely girl and Im so pleased shes achieved so much this term. All of Sarahs teacher's are delighted with her academic results' and as her form teacher Im particularly happy with her contribution's to school life. Sarahs' perfor-mance in the school play was admirable and wer'e very lucky to have her on the cricket team. Well done, Sarah!*
Im afraid Adolf has not had a good year at Winston Boys. Hes determined to make life as difficult as possible for all those around him. Ive spoken to him on several occasion's about his attitude and behaviour but hes apparently unconcerned about the consequences of his action's. Hes failed all subjects this year and been suspended three times. If Adolfs performance does not improve next term, Il'l have no choice but to recommend his expulsion.	*Mrs Rodger's and I are quite pleased with Georginas progress so far. Shes settled into kinder quickly and seem's to be enjoying herself. Georginas verbal skills are excellent although weve noticed that shes reluctant to assert herself. Were also slightly concerned that shes failed to master the alphabet, however theres still plenty of time before well consider it a problem. Perhap's some practice at home wouldnt go astray. Overall, wed say Georginas coping well with kindergarten.*

GRAMMAR UNIT 18 COMMAS, COLONS AND SEMI-COLONS (REVISION/PRACTICE)

Commas mark a pause in a sentence. They separate similar parts of speech and items in a list. They also mark phrases and clauses. Commas separate direct speech from the rest of a sentence and can act like a pair of brackets.

Colons introduce lists, quotations and definitions. They also join two parts of a sentence, where the second part explains or elaborates on the first.

Semi-colons are used to join two complete sentences that are closely related. They can also be used to break up long, complicated lists.

1 Place commas in the appropriate places in these sentences.

- **a** After we left Croatia we travelled through Slovenia Italy Switzerland and France.
- **b** 'Oh sorry' said Ethan 'I didn't realise anyone was in here.'
- **c** Place the flour milk eggs and half the sugar into a small mixing bowl.
- **d** Before deciding what to do we had to agree on where we were going.

2 Make these sentences grammatically correct by removing some punctuation marks and inserting colons.

- **a** Martha's list of complaints was long. She was a very fussy woman.

  ____

- **b** Silence that dreadful bell, it frightens the animals.

  ____

- **c** Who said, 'Good night, good night! Parting is such sweet sorrow'?

  ____

- **d** It was quite obvious what Ian thought about lending me the money; no way!

  ____

3 Two of these sentences contain correctly placed semi-colons. Place a tick beside the correct sentences.

- **a** Duncan dashed off to return library books; while I sat in the car and waited.
- **b** Dean failed his end of year maths exam; his parents were pretty disappointed.
- **c** All the bugs; lizards; rodents; snakes and tiny mammals died of the same disease.
- **d** Lucy was embarrassed about the bandages; they looked pretty silly.

4 Put commas, colons or semi-colons into these sentences.

- **a** Wiping the grimy sweat from his brow Terry continued to dig deeper and deeper.
- **b** Dad wanted us to do several jobs while we were on holidays clean the pool finish making the dog's kennel chop firewood and put up the Christmas lights.
- **c** Before departing this morning you will each receive the following a back-pack a map covering the entire search area two full water bottles which may be re-filled at any time food for the day a whistle and most importantly a first aid kit.
- **d** I want one of these cars an XJ8 Jaguar in British racing green a red or black Porsche Boxster with black leather trim a fire-engine red 1969 Cadillac with clean white leather upholstery or one of those sleek sexy new Lamborghinis in a bright metallic blue.

GRAMMAR UNIT 19 PUNCTUATING SENTENCES (PRACTICE)

This unit allows you an opportunity to practise all of your punctuation skills.

1 **Punctuate the following sentences correctly.**

a Mrs Knowles how do you spell sciamachy Julie asked her English teacher

b Oh no I groaned to Pat as I looked at todays date. I forgot my Dads birthday

c Curses like chickens come home to roost

d You muttered Cynthia are determined to ruin my party Frank Why

e You cover Trevor Street Tin Road Alma Avenue and Foster Parade Ill do Taylors Reserve Smith Street and up Flint Road to Bobs fish and chips shop Got that

f The dog jumped into the filthy polluted pond and then shook its wet slimy stinking coat all over us

g Trixie swung her stun gun around and fired at the approaching beasts

h Polonius most useful piece of advice This above all to thine own self be true

i Gladys Green president of the Flashy Meadows Tennis Club was proud of the clubs hundred year history its new clubhouse the immaculately maintained courts with their state of the art scoreboards and despite the recent controversy the clubs membership policy

2 **Imagine that your younger brother or sister has asked you to check some homework. You feel generous and offer to help rewrite it. (Hint: use paragraphs, capital letters, commas, colons, hyphens, question marks, exclamation marks, quotation marks and full stops.)**

godfrey was a grumpy old goat he was grumpy morning noon and night godfrey would lie under the shade of a big tree munch on dandelions and think of what he could grump about happy young goats would trot up to him and ask him to play go away! he'd growl I'm grumpy other old goats would often amble up and ask him to accompany them on their walks no, he'd grumble I'm too grumpy one day as he lay in the shade chewing on dandelions Godfrey felt lonely and looked around him beyond the shade of the tree he saw happy little goats frolicking in the long grass along the well worn dirt tracks he saw groups of contented old goats strolling and chattering I've had enough of being grumpy he thought it's left me lonely and bitter i'm going to stop being grumpy from now on he got up wandered tentatively out of the shade and approached the frolicking young kids may I join you he asked no they shouted back you're too grumpy to play godfrey then stopped a group of chattering goats may I walk with you he asked politely no they quickly answered you're too grumpy to walk with us godfrey was crestfallen he was so disappointed and sad he wandered back to his dandelions under the tree lay down and felt sorry for himself i've been too grumpy for too long he realised everyone's given up on me.

the moral of this story if you're an old goat don't be grumpy

GRAMMAR UNIT 20 DIRECT SPEECH

GRAMMAR

Direct speech is the *actual* words spoken by someone. Indirect speech is what someone is *reported* to have said or thought.

Direct speech: 'Do you think they liked my presentation?' asked Ursula.

Indirect speech: Ursula wondered whether they liked her presentation.

If you need a reminder about how to punctuate direct speech accurately, look at units 29, 30 and 31 in Book 1.

1 Place quotation marks around the direct speech in these sentences.

a The pub, Dietmar growled, is the last place you should be right now.

b Oh, said Jenni casually, I never go to doctors. I don't believe in them.

c Look! wept Maria bitterly. Look at what they've done to my garden.

d We'll ring the police, declared Andy, and let them sort it out.

e Disapproval froze Jade's face like a block. I can't believe, she said, you just did that!

2 Punctuate these sentences correctly.

a The real reason said Fiona quietly is that I have simply had enough

b You snarled Phoebe are a dirty slimy little rodent

c I think it's a bit pricey Peter said to Matt What do you think

d This is not so hard thought Kathleen Why haven't I tried this before

e I'm petrified of failing confided Lucy to Brett Aren't you worried about it at all

f You can go in now Miss Petrasevic called the receptionist He's ready to see you

g This thought Daniel is going to push her over the edge

h I pulled a chair around so I could see her face properly You shouldn't underestimate your talents Sophie You're a fabulous dancer

i Have you got a hankie asked Ruth's mother You always forget your hankie

3 Rewrite this text, creating paragraphs and punctuating correctly.

Okay folks listen in please My name is Derek and I'm taking your class photo this year so I'm going to need lots of cooperation and lots of smiles What a dork whispered Arinta Yeh whispered back Rosa Derek the dork No talking up the back thanks girls called dorky Derek Sorry Derek Arinta called back We were just thinking about what would make us smile Well said Derek You could think about making your parents happy with a nice class photo for Christmas Oh man sighed Arinta this dude's a double dork

4 Write a dialogue between two people. Choose one of the following scenarios and ensure you create paragraphs and punctuate accurately:

- a police officer pulling over a driver for speeding
- an interview between a reporter and the lead singer of a popular rock group
- a conversation between a doctor and a nervous patient

GRAMMAR UNIT 21 PHRASES

A **phrase** is a group of words that does not contain a finite verb and cannot stand alone. Phrases can do the job of nouns, adjectives or adverbs. Phrases are added to sentences to provide extra information or to make the sentence more interesting. Phrases can be at the beginning, in the middle or at the end of sentences.

Noun phrase: *The old man next door* is very lonely.

Adjectival phrase: I thought Sean Connery, *that handsome Scottish actor*, was the best James Bond.

Adverbial phrase: The speeding car plunged *over the cliff*.

1 Are these groups of words sentences or phrases?

a She walked up the street. __________

b Up the street. __________

c My beautiful sister. __________

d My beautiful sister turned six last week. __________

e It is nine o'clock. __________

f What's for dinner? __________

g In the bath. __________

h The pianist was excellent. __________

i Covered in snow. __________

j The bees hummed. __________

2 Underline the phrases in these sentences.

a Annabelle, Rachel and Lara, my best friends from high school, will be my bridesmaids.

b Timothy was approached by an odd-looking man in a dirty brown trench coat.

c John parked the wheelbarrow under the house.

d When it's dark, I'll light the candles.

e I love eating chocolate in the bath.

3 Are these groups of words *noun*, *adjectival* or *adverbial* phrases?

a a beautiful woman __________

b wearing a purple scarf __________

c behind the shelter sheds __________

d into the ocean __________

e the world's greatest liar __________

f after the party __________

g covered in bright yellow flowers __________

h a mutant mouse __________

i for him __________

j under a smooth grey stone __________

k empty and dilapidated __________

GRAMMAR UNIT 22 CLAUSES

GRAMMAR

A **clause** is a group of words containing a subject and a finite verb. It is usually part of a larger sentence.

A **main clause** (or **principal clause**) can stand alone, and will make sense as a complete thought. It contains the most important information in the sentence.

Rick tidied his bedroom because his father paid him pocket money on a Saturday.

A **subordinate clause** cannot stand alone. It will not make sense by itself and needs to be joined to the main clause. It is usually joined by conjunctions, such as *because*, *before*, *until*, *when*, *while*, *if* and *after*. A subordinate clause gives more information about the main clause.

main clause	*subordinate clause*
The rowers were thrilled	when their boat crossed the finishing line.
subordinate clause	*main clause*
Because her mother cried out,	Rachel thought there must be an intruder in the garden.

1 Underline the main clause in each sentence.

a When Minette opened the fridge she could feel the cold air.

b Tracey followed her dog because he was sniffing along the edge of the fence.

c Larry was fuming because his well-intentioned plan had failed.

d While Jake distracted the sales assistant, Jo slipped the perfume into her handbag.

e If you invite Theresa to your party, I'm not going to come.

2 Underline the subordinate clauses in each sentence. (There may be more than one.)

a Fran pushed open the door with her foot because her arms were full of groceries.

b Although rent was cheap, it was a mistake to move to the city during the Great Depression because it wasn't possible to grow vegetables any more.

c Shane enjoys fantasy novels as they provide relief from the boring reality of everyday life.

d J. Edgar Hoover, Director of the FBI, died in 1972.

e Even though he refused to do any preparation, David still managed to pass his learner's permit test.

3 Complete each sentence with a subordinate clause.

a Troy didn't think anyone would notice ______________________________

b ______________________________ she put her school bag on the floor.

c During summer, ______________________________ the trees all died.

d ______________________________ Liam ran out into the rain.

e Mr Taylor, ______________________________, is an inspiration to us all.

f ______________________________ they missed the train.

g The audience was stunned ______________________________.

h ______________________________, we can't be friends.

GRAMMAR UNIT 23 SYNONYMS

A **synonym** is a word with almost the same meaning as another word.

bad: *inferior*, *poor*, *rotten*, *vile*, *wicked*

When you replace a word with a synonym, make sure it is the same part of speech. For example, if you wish to replace an adjective with a synonym, ensure the new word is an adjective also.

Synonyms may be used to make writing more interesting, or to make the meaning of a sentence clearer and more precise.

After heavy rain, the dry bed of Lake Eyre becomes a *big* body of water.

After heavy rain, the dry bed of Lake Eyre becomes a *great/vast/enormous/immense* body of water.

1 Match each adjective with the appropriate synonym.

Adjective	Synonym
1 unlucky	___ unwell
2 noisy	___ unfortunate
3 sick	___ excellent
4 busy	___ loud
5 terrific	___ hectic

Adjective	Synonym
1 dirty	___ autocratic
2 despotic	___ audacious
3 unsightly	___ powerless
4 bold	___ indecent
5 helpless	___ repulsive

2 List some synonyms for each of the following words.

a push ______________________________

b tempting ______________________________

c gentle ______________________________

d factual ______________________________

e shrewd ______________________________

f nice ______________________________

g walking ______________________________

h scared ______________________________

i clever ______________________________

j tenacity ______________________________

3 Rewrite the following sentences, replacing the underlined words with a more interesting synonym.

a He knew from the <u>start</u> that he wouldn't <u>like</u> the film.

b A prize was <u>given</u> to Dr Quinn for his research into <u>groups</u> of tropical insects.

c In order for this <u>plan</u> to be a success, we must be <u>alert</u>.

d Curled up inside the <u>curly</u> leaves of the lettuce lay a <u>shocked</u> caterpillar.

e The <u>big</u>, <u>angry</u> bandicoot <u>growled</u> at the <u>scared</u> echidna.

f Advertisements on television are often <u>boring</u> and <u>annoying</u>.

g We can expect <u>heavy</u> rain, <u>heavy</u> winds and <u>heavy</u> damage when the twister hits.

h My <u>good</u> friend Peter is a <u>good</u> baseball player.

GRAMMAR UNIT 24 ANTONYMS

GRAMMAR

An **antonym** is a word with an opposite meaning to a given word.

Cold is the antonym of *hot*.

Antonyms are often completely different from the other word.

always/never | heavy/light | strong/weak | negative/affirmative | safe/dangerous
mouldy/fresh | cherish/neglect | dull/vivid

Sometimes, however, adding a prefix or suffix to the original word forms the antonym.

plug/unplug | adequate/inadequate | agree/disagree | harm/harmless

The word *antonym* is derived from the prefix *anti-*, which means 'against'.

1 Match each word with its antonym.

1 robust	___ reward
2 punish	___ generous
3 mean	___ twisted
4 full	___ flimsy
5 straight	___ empty

1 passive	___ defeat
2 victory	___ barren
3 timid	___ preserve
4 fruitful	___ active
5 annihilate	___ fearless

2 Think of an antonym for each of these words.

a old ____________
b maximum ____________
c coarse ____________
d late ____________
e absence ____________
f arrival ____________
g sell ____________
h forget ____________
i mourn ____________
j birth ____________

3 Rewrite these sentences, replacing the underlined words with an antonym.

a The difference in the bill was obvious when they started to <u>save</u> water.

____

b After the <u>short</u> operation, Sue's leg was <u>better</u>.

____

c The councillors were <u>satisfied</u> with the architect's ideas for the <u>new</u> courthouse.

____

d Joachim was <u>elated</u> with the results of his final engineering exams.

____

e The book by Frederick Maxwell, <u>formerly</u> a professor at the university, was published last month and received <u>poor</u> reviews in the local paper.

____

____

4 Add a prefix or suffix to the following words to form an antonym.

a responsible ____________
b sense ____________
c construct ____________
d advantage ____________
e cloudy ____________
f relent ____________

GRAMMAR UNIT 25 HOMONYMS

A **homonym** is a word that is spelt the same as another but is actually a completely different word with a different meaning.

bill (bird's beak)	*bill* (statement of charges)
soil (dirt)	*soil* (to stain or make dirty)
bank (side of a river)	*bank* (place where money is kept)

If you need to use a homonym, ensure its meaning is clear: you must avoid ambiguity.

1 Give a definition of the homonyms underlined in these sentences.

a The petrol tanker swerved out of control, hit a small tree then slid down a bank. ______

b Hakan rows on Saturdays and studies on Sundays. ______

c We had to till the soil before we could plant the seeds. ______

d Patricia's nagging and whinging was hard to bear. ______

e My expectations and your performance are poles apart. ______

2 Now go back and write sentences containing the homonyms, but this time using their other meanings.

3 Circle all of the homonyms in the following sentences.

a Every Sunday night Grandpa cuts his toenails and files the corn on his foot.

b The entrée was a lovely soup of chicken and pulses.

c Luke's favourite chill out music was R and B and soul.

d The union bargained for fair and reasonable contracts and a general pay rise.

e Our trip to the beach was a failure as the waves were not big enough to surf.

4 Find the thirteen homonyms in this word search.

K	I	N	D	Z	D	E	A	R
R	O	W	M	E	O	E	P	E
A	S	Q	S	X	V	G	R	D
B	A	T	L	A	S	R	E	R
X	F	R	W	C	C	A	S	O
U	E	I	I	T	K	V	S	O
I	M	P	L	E	M	E	N	T

5 Choose three of the homonyms you found in the word search and write two sentences showing you understand the word's different meanings.

GRAMMAR UNIT 26 PREFIXES

A **prefix** is a word element placed at the front of a word (the *stem* or *root*) to form a completely new word. (*Pre* means 'before' in Latin.)

discolour: *dis-* is the prefix, *-colour* is the stem or root

Prefixes alter the meaning of the stem word. In this example, the prefix *dis-* negates the stem word *colour*. So *discolour* means 'to ruin or destroy a colour'.

Prefixes are usually derived from Latin or Greek and have a meaning of their own.

Prefix	Meaning	Examples
a-	on, out, up	aboard, ashore,
ad-	to, towards	adhere, adhesive
ante-	before	antecedent, antechamber
anti-	against	antiseptic, antibiotic, antidote
auto-	self	automatic, autobiography
bi-	two, twice	bicycle, bisect, bilingual
co-, com-, con-	together, with	cooperate, combine, connect

Prefix	Meaning	Examples
contra-	against	contradict, contrast, contrary
de-	down, from, away	descend, depart, decrease
dia-	through or across	dialogue, diagonal, diagram
ex-	former	ex-captain, ex-student
extra-	beyond	extraordinary, extravagant
fore-	before, in front of	forefront, foremost, foresee
hemi-	half	hemisphere, hemicycle

1 Circle the prefix in each of the following words.

a untidy
b inaccurate
c misled
d impolite
e disobey
f unnecessary
g superego
h aloft
i semicolon
j homophone
k expel
l demitasse

2 Give examples of words that use the following prefixes.

a ab-/abs- (*away from*) ____________________
b arch- (*chief*) ____________________
c bene- (*well*) ____________________
d cata- (*down*) ____________________
e circum- (*around*) ____________________
f epi- (*upon*) ____________________
g hypo- (*under*) ____________________
h inter- (*between*) ____________________
i non- (*not*) ____________________
j para- (*beside*) ____________________

3 Add a prefix to the following stem words. Then write the meaning of the new word.

a ______________arm ____
b ______________terrestrial ____
c ______________centenary ____
d ______________natal ____
e ______________pilot ____
f ______________clockwise ____

GRAMMAR UNIT 27 SUFFIXES

Suffixes are exactly the same as prefixes except they are placed at the *end* of stem words. The addition of a suffix often means the stem word must be altered slightly.

pretty prett*ily* sedate sedative metal metallic

Here are some common suffixes:

Suffix	Meaning	Examples
-able, -ible	capable of being	delectable, sensible
-an, -ean, -ian	belonging to or relating to	Christian, Jacobean, Italian
-ance, -ence	state of	endurance, dependence
-ant, -ent	one who	informant, assistant, student
-ary	place where a thing is kept	mortuary, library, granary
-ative	tending to	talkative
-craft	skill	handicraft, witchcraft

Suffix	Meaning	Examples
-dom	state, rank or domain	kingdom, freedom
-eer, -er, -ier, -or	person engaged in a trade or profession	engineer, teacher, courier, doctor
-en, -et, -ette	little	maiden, minuet, cigarette
-en	made of	golden, woollen
-ess	female	goddess, temptress
-fold	multiplied by	threefold
-ful	full of	beautiful, pitiful

1 Underline the suffix in each of these words.

a stupidly **f** certainty **k** driver **p** sisterhood
b avoidable **g** twofold **l** friendly **q** builder
c buses **h** African **m** criticism **r** bushcraft
d coldest **i** eastward **n** critical **s** artist
e lengthwise **j** certainly **o** powerful **t** hopeless

2 Add a suffix to these stems to form a new word.

a new ________ **e** infirm ________
b joy ________ **f** sustain ________
c attend ________ **g** wood ________
d seam ________ **h** inquire ________

3 Provide examples of words that use the following suffixes.

a -craft ________ **e** -ist ________
b -ative ________ **f** -wise ________
c -ess ________ **g** -teen ________
d -ly ________ **h** -ful ________

4 Identify the stem for each of these words.

a businesslike ________ **f** postage ________
b confirmed ________ **g** registrar ________
c emancipation ________ **h** rover ________
d negation ________ **i** oceanic ________
e financial ________ **j** yielding ________

GRAMMAR UNIT 28 USING A DICTIONARY

GRAMMAR

A **dictionary** is amazingly useful. It provides you with an enormous range of information. You can:

Find out how to spell words by looking up the first few letters alphabetically.
Discover the meaning of words.
Check to which part of speech a word belongs.
Determine how to pronounce a word.
Check how to employ a word accurately.
With some dictionaries you can learn other information, such as the origin of a word and its history.

1 How do you spell these words? Use your dictionary to fill in the gaps.

a corn_______pia
b smor_______bord
c pneu_______a
d sag_______i_______
e Aa_______
f feather_______t
g kad_______
h anon_______o_______
i om_______an
j misan_______ope

2 What part of speech is each of the following words? Use your dictionary to check your answers.

a regurgitate _______
b exposition _______
c comestible _______
d mealy _______
e talon _______
f foreshadow _______
g plagiarise _______
h nepotism _______
i thwack _______
j infatuated _______

3 What is ...

a trumpery? _______
b a wobbegong? _______
____
c a coup? _______
d a prodigy? _______
e an aardvark? _______

4 Use your dictionary to answer the following questions.

a What does a *theodolite* measure? _______
b Is Mata Hari a woman or a man? _______
c What is *Qantas* the abbreviation of? _______
____
d Where would you find a kibbutz? _______
e Is zymase an enzyme or a thick-walled spore? _______
f Where would you come from if you spoke Esperanto? _______
g Where would you find greenbacks? _______
h What does *sang-froid* mean in English? _______
i Is the Transvaal in South Africa or Europe? _______

GRAMMAR UNIT 29 USING A THESAURUS

A **thesaurus** is a book that lists words in groups of synonyms. It helps writers to find alternatives to overused or uninteresting words. To use a thesaurus, look up the word you wish to replace. (A thesaurus will either list words in alphabetical order or have an index of words.) Look carefully at all the synonyms provided. Think about the context in which the word will be used and make sure that you understand what the synonym means before you use it. Also, make sure that your new word belongs to the same part of speech as the old one. You cannot replace a noun with an adjective, for example.

If you looked up *powerful* in a thesaurus, you would probably find synonyms like: *mighty*, *potent*, *strapping*, *strong*, *sturdy*, *vigorous*, *authoritative*, *commanding*, *dominant* and *influential*. You can see that although these are all synonyms, they do not all mean exactly the same thing. Therefore you would have to choose one that is perfect for your particular sentence.

1 Use a thesaurus to find synonyms for each of these words.

a hunk ______

b charter ______

c tolerant ______

d affable ______

e bleach ______

f nag ______

g romantic ______

2 Replace each of the underlined words with a more interesting synonym.

a I bought a nice new dress. ______

b It was a long, boring night. ______

c The carpenter did a good job. ______

d Dad cooked us a nice meal. ______

e Unfortunately we had to stop our lessons. ______

f Libby wore the most sensational red lipstick. ______

g Do you understand the enormity of the situation? ______

h That was a nasty stunt to pull. ______

i I've had such a bad day! ______

j We encountered a big, scary monster. ______

3 Use a thesaurus to match the words on the left with their synonym on the right.

1 peevish	____ armistice
2 hot	____ pseudo
3 truce	____ congenial
4 blithe	____ cheerful
5 agreeable	____ querulous
6 phoney	____ sultry

4 Write a short imaginative piece of writing about one of the following things. Use a thesaurus to improve the quality of your writing.

- the adventures of an amorous aardvark
- the disappointments of a depressed dingo

GRAMMAR UNIT 30 COMMON MISTAKES: HAVE/OF

GRAMMAR

Have is a *verb*, which is an action word. It is part of the infinitive *to have*.

Present tense: I *have*, you *have*, he *has*, she *has*, it *has*, they *have*, we *have*

Past tense: I *had*, you *had*, he *had*, she *had*, it *had*, they *had*, we *had*

Of is a *preposition*. It links nouns or pronouns with other parts of speech.

A bag *of* rice. Six *of* those please. *Of* course you can!

Of should *never* be used instead of *have* in constructions, such as '*You should not have*'. There is often confusion about this because in casual, rapid speech, the two words can sound similar. Some people make the error of writing things such as '*she could of if she tried*'. This is incorrect and does not make sense. Some people also make the mistake of thinking that *should've* stands for *should of*. It does not: it is an abbreviation of *should have*.

You should be aware that contractions such as *should've* and *would've* are only used in speech, not formal writing. When writing, you should use the words in full: *should have* or *would have*.

1 What do the following contractions mean?

a could've ____________

b should've ____________

c might've ____________

d what've ____________

e how've ____________

f had've ____________

2 *Have* or *of*? Fill in the gap in each sentence with the correct word.

a 'You should ________ seen the fish that got away, Mum!' shouted little Johnny.

b 'May I have another one ________ your lovely biscuits?' asked Maeve.

c Two ________ the escaped prisoners were recaptured by police last night.

d I could ________ hit that woman.

e I would not ________ picked you as a gambling man.

3 Complete each of these sentences by inserting one word. (It may be a contraction.)

a If you had ____________ done as you were told, we wouldn't be in this mess.

b 'I ____________ been a professional jockey, if I wasn't so tall,' declared Tim.

c '____________ you done to my hair?' shrieked the distraught woman.

d 'How ____________ you coped since you lost the butler?' Jenny asked Diedre.

e ____________ all the people one could meet in Outer Mongolia, we ran into the bloke from next door!

f Our local councillors ____________ given up trying to remove graffiti.

g 'I reckon Stevie ____________ nicked your bike,' whispered Danny.

h 'We will ____________ a party to end all parties!' declared Mr Griswold.

i Harry should ____________ allowed more time to get there.

j I guess I could ____________ tried harder.

k We ____________ sold the gold before prices slumped. We ____________ made a fortune.

Grammar Unit 31 Common Mistakes: Me, Myself and I

Me, **myself** and **I** are personal pronouns that refer to the speaker of the sentence. That is, they are **first person pronouns**. The choice of pronoun is decided by its place in a sentence.

I is used when the pronoun is the subject in the sentence (nominative case).

I like to watch TV.

Me is used when the pronoun is the object in the sentence (objective case).

He hit *me*.

Myself is a reflexive pronoun. It is the object in a sentence and refers to the subject.

I cut *myself*.

Myself is also used after prepositions.

I poured the water over *myself*.

These rules apply even when there is more than one subject or object.

He and *I* are good buddies.

The shadow fell across Jenny and *me*.

I bought drinks for Jake and *myself*.

Notice how the pronoun referring to the person speaking is always placed last.

1 Fill in the gaps with *me*, *myself* or *I*.

a The teacher was pleased that __________ had finished my work so quickly.

b Sandra and __________ took the children to the swimming pool.

c __________ banged on the door and asked them to help __________.

d Since cutting __________ on glass, __________ always wear thongs at the beach.

e Please don't look at __________ like that; __________ feel intimidated.

f '__________ would rather go to the bank __________, thank you.'

g Jane and __________ were good friends before she stole my boyfriend.

h Uncle Bob gave Frank and __________ a very stern lecture when he found us.

i Dad and __________ love fishing, although he is always luckier than __________.

j __________ blame __________.

2 Change the underlined pronoun to the appropriate first person pronoun.

After the operation she expected to be able to see perfectly but it took longer than she expected. She had to train herself to remember where everything was in the kitchen so that she could make herself a cup of tea. In the bathroom everything had to be exactly right so she could brush her teeth and wash herself. In the shower, she put the shampoo on the floor and the conditioner on the shelf, but every few days she had to remind herself which was which. It came as a surprise to her, how much the restricted vision affected her.

3 Write an imaginative piece about one of the following topics. Write in the first person and concentrate on the correct use of *me*, *myself* and *I*.

- The day I decided to take control of my life …
- I once made the mistake of trusting my sister …
- My life would not be complete without my iPod …
- I suspect my obsession with saving water is getting out of hand …

GRAMMAR UNIT 32 COMMON MISTAKES: IT'S AND ITS

If you can master the **it's/its** issue, then you will be the champion of the world!

It's is short for *it is*. It is called a contraction, because it is the abbreviated version of *it is*.

It's a nice day. *It's* raining. *It's* a disaster. *It's* such a shame. Don't you think *it's* unfair?

Its is a possessive pronoun like *my*, *your*, *his*, *her* and *their*. It shows ownership or possession.

The dog wagged *its* tail. The lion protected *its* cub. The box fell on *its* side.

If you are ever in doubt as to which to use, then carry out a little test: can you say *it is*? If using *it is* makes sense, then you should write *it's*. Look at these examples:

It's a very cloudy day. (*It is* a very cloudy day.)	This makes sense, therefore *it's* is correct.
The rose was at *it's* best. (The rose was at *it is* best.)	This does not make sense. It should be: The rose was at *its* best.

1 Circle the correct word in these sentences.

a Pass me the remote control. Its/It's on the bench.

b When operating a chainsaw its/it's imperative to wear safety equipment.

c The bee buzzed around the lavender, then returned to its/it's nest.

d It's/Its much easier to juggle than you think.

e Can we get rid of this old table? Its/It's painted the most awful brown.

f We told the kids the story about a leopard that lost its/it's spots.

g The cat battered open the door of its/it's cage and ran for its/it's life.

h It's/its pointless to hope that it's/its over.

i Jamaica is a Caribbean country. Its/It's a member of the Commonwealth. Kingston is its/it's capital.

j I can't think of its/it's title. Its/It's on the tip of my tongue, but its/it's eluding me.

2 This text contains twelve incorrectly used *it's* and *its*. Rewrite it correctly.

To operate the remote-controlled car, turn the main switch to 'on'. Its located on the underside of the vehicle. Its important to regularly check this switch as it's easy to leave on and waste the batteries. Its also important to remove the antenna from the vehicle while not in operation as its quite fragile and easily damaged. It's storage container is located on the left side of the carry case. To recharge batteries, place the vehicle on its right side, remove the battery hatch (its located near the left rear wheel) and plug the recharging cord into the receiver. Its imperative that the batteries are not charged until its obvious they are completely dead. This vehicle is designed for heavy use. Its also designed for rough and uneven terrain, but its not suitable in water. We know you will have fun with your car: experts have designed it's features, so its easy to guarantee your satisfaction!

GRAMMAR UNIT 33 SOME CONFUSING WORDS

There are many words in the English language that cause confusion. Here are some of them:

Word	Part of speech	Meaning	Synonyms	Example
accept	verb	consent to receive	take, receive	We *accept* your invitation.
except	preposition	not including, other than	apart from, excluding	Everyone danced *except* Kylie.
affect	verb	act on, move feelings	alter, change, influence	The accident will *affect* us all.
effect	noun	the result of an action	consequence, outcome, result	The lights created a pretty *effect*.
effect	verb	bring about or accomplish	achieve, cause, produce	We'll need to *effect* big changes.
bought	verb	past tense of *to buy*	purchased, paid for	I *bought* it in Myer.
brought	verb	past tense of *to bring*	carried, provided, gave	He *brought* great joy to others.
chose	verb	past tense of *to choose*	picked, wanted	We *chose* our subjects last month.
choose	verb	decide, select, take	pick, want, prefer, wish	I *choose* not to smoke.

1 Circle the correct word to complete these sentences. (Be careful!)

a Make sure you choose/chose your colours carefully.
b You should not underestimate the affect/effect this is going to have on the staff.
c I will accept/except your offer of help only if I can return the favour.
d Last year I choose/chose to stay home on New Year's Eve.
e Some movies can affect/effect children's behaviour.
f Accept/Except for Portia, we all received pay rises.
g He bought/brought it at a reduced price.

2 Fill in the gaps with one of the 'confusing words' from the table above. Words may be used more than once.

a It's lucky that I ____________ my umbrella along: it's pouring!
b I knew Linda would not ____________ my apology.
c Why don't you wear the dress I ____________ for your birthday?
d The long-term ____________s of drug abuse are well documented.
e The ____________ this may have on our children is just too difficult to predict.
f If I have a choice, then I ____________ you!
g I had a choice and I ____________ you!
h Brittany forgot her decision would ____________ everyone.

3 Create another table to show the difference between these pairs of confusing words: dependant/dependent, of/off and weather/whether.

34 MORE CONFUSING WORDS

Word	Part of speech	Meaning	Synonyms	Example
allowed	verb	granted permission	permitted, approved	Mrs Dean *allowed* us to leave early.
aloud	adverb	loudly, audibly	clearly, distinctly	I hate being asked to read *aloud*.
fewer	adverb	less than expected or before		There were *fewer* people at the conference than last year.
less	various	smaller in number or size	little, smaller	I'd like to eat *less* red meat.
uninterested	adjective	not interested	bored, unexcited	I am entirely *uninterested* in boxing.
disinterested	adjective	not influenced by one's own advantage	impartial, unbiased, unprejudiced	As a judge, it is important to remain *disinterested* and unemotional.
hung	verb	past tense of *hang*	dangled, covered, draped, fixed	We *hung* out the clothes before it rained.
hanged	verb	suspended from the neck until dead	killed, murdered	Ned Kelly was *hanged* at Old Melbourne Gaol.

1 Circle the correct word in these sentences.

a Some people would like to see murderers hanged/hung for their crimes.

b Dad was less/fewer than impressed with my exam results.

c To be a good juror you must be disinterested/uninterested in the outcome.

d I am only allowed/aloud to leave the table when the meal is finished.

e When companies go bankrupt, shareholders are hanged/hung out to dry.

f Because Marcy was uninterested/disinterested in hockey, she read instead.

g The protesters hung/hanged their banner over the embassy gates.

2 Demonstrate your understanding of all eight of the 'confusing words' in the table above by using each one correctly in a sentence.

Spelling Spelling Spelling Spel

Spelling

JUDY CONLAN AND MARIE HENLEY

As well as consolidating spelling skills, this section teaches the use of words in context in a more intensive way than recognition of words in prose studies. Seen as equally important is the need to stimulate interest in, and awareness of, language skills. To this end, the thirty-four units have been injected with humour wherever possible to avoid the tedium so often inherent in this kind of learning experience.

Traditional methods have been used throughout, such as spelling rules, exercises involving recognition of parts of speech and punctuation usage, and creative writing exercises, based on vocabulary used in the units. Vocabulary has been repeated constantly — in the spelling lists, instructions and exercises — so word recognition becomes more confident.

SPELLING UNIT 1 GAUGING YOUR ABILITY

gauge	ignition	metallic	major
lubricate	complaint	level	mishap
liquor	ventilation	cheque	financial
adjust	grease	liable	cashier
penetrate	transaction	panel	mileage

1 Find appropriate forms of the words listed that mean:

grease ____________ lighting, act of starting combustion ____________

cause air to circulate ____________ indicator ____________

subject to ____________ pierce ____________

accident ____________ most important ____________

2 Match these sentence halves:

Many a motoring mishap occurs	are paid by cheque.
Adequate ventilation is	so we can work out our petrol consumption.
Most large financial transactions	to the ignition switch.
You should not drink	essential when travelling in a car.
The complaint about the cheque	alcohol when driving.
An adjustment had to be made	was passed on to the cashier.
Keep a record of our mileage	on greasy roads.

3 Complete these sentence fragments:

Metallic machines are liable to rust if ____________________________________

A serious complaint had been levelled against ____________________________________

Wood panelling ____________________________________

Regular lubrication of engine parts is necessary to ____________________________________

Penetrating the dense forest ____________________________________

It is difficult to gauge ____________________________________

The majority of ____________________________________

Lightning can ignite ____________________________________

4 Find the correct forms of words from the list, opposite in meaning to:

extinguish ____________ minority ____________ praise ____________

5 List as many adjectives as you can describing the nature of materials: e.g.,
metallic, ____________________________________

6 You are a robot, involved in a collision with another robot. Write the dialogue that would ensue if a complaint was to be heard by a panel convened to hear the case. Use as many of the words from the list as you can.

____

____

____

____

____

____

SPELLING UNIT 2 HOPEFULLY I AM TRAVELLING TO ...

faithful	grateful	hopeful	skilful
useful	resourceful	penniless	loneliness
clumsily	guiltily	tunnelled	controlled
travelled	quarrelled	worshipped	permitted
committed	within	forgotten	forbidden

1 Use list words to complete these sentences:

The ______________ horse stopped beside its fallen master.

So ______________ was he at manoeuvring the car around the corners, that he won easily.

'I'm busy, so please try to make yourself ______________,' said her mother.

He was surprisingly ______________ when stranded on the island.

______________ for her assistance, the man rewarded his daughter.

He was ______________ some news would arrive that day.

She ____________ constantly with her younger brother.

The traveller was stranded, ______________, in Singapore.

______________, she fumbled with the lock.

The little boy crept ______________ from the kitchen.

______________ is a big problem for outback families.

2 What does the word *non-committal* mean? Use it in a sentence:

____

____

3 Circle the jarring word:

affluent, penniless, impecunious, needy

ingenious, imaginative, responsive, resourceful

solitude, loneliness, desolation, ecstasy

awkwardly, aggressively, clumsily, incompetently

appreciative, informative, thankful, grateful

devoted, faithful, loyal, unblemished

4 Change each of these words by adding one of the following suffixes: *-ed*, *-en* or *-est*:

control ____________	forbid ____________	worship ____________
commit ____________	write ____________	permit ____________
travel ____________	forgot ____________	cruel ____________

5 Here is the beginning of a nonsense rhyme; complete it:

A robbery he had committed,
The traveller sourly admitted,
But it could not be permitted,
____

SPELLING

SPELLING UNIT 3 THE LONG ARM OF THE LAW

arrest	offence	conviction	guilty
innocent	justice	officer	traffic
assumed	summons	criminal	jury
illegal	breach	magistrate	solution
civil	detain	appeal	uniform

1 Use a word from the word list to complete the following sentences:

It is ____________ to drive a car faster than the speed limit.

Speed limits in suburban areas are ____________ throughout Australia.

Any ____________ of the law can result in a ____________ being issued.

When speeding fines are not paid, you are required to appear before a ____________ in court.

Following a criminal's ____________, he/she must appear in court.

To ensure ____________ is carried out, a person is ____________ innocent until proved guilty.

A ____________ determines the guilt or innocence of people accused of serious crimes.

A person can appeal against a ____________.

____________ cases are not tried in the same courts as criminal cases.

2 Now see if you can use some of the words in different contexts:

You must be ____________ when addressing teachers.

A ____________ in the dam wall led to disastrous floods.

You must have the courage of your ____________.

To ____________ the spread of the disease, large numbers of cattle were destroyed.

____________ are worn by most students in secondary schools.

That joke really ____________ to my sense of humour.

I am late because I was ____________ at the dentist.

3 Match these columns:

assume	displease
advise	excuse
offend	trade
convict	lawful
summon	attractive
justify	prisoner
appealing	counsel (suggest)
detain	suppose
traffic	command
legal	arrest

4 Have a mock trial of a student convicted of riding his/her horse through a red light.

SPELLING UNIT 4 PREVENTION IS BETTER THAN CURE

spirits	methylated	poisonous	implements
disinfectant	detergent	electrocution	convalescent
kerosene	contamination	nutrition	elimination
digestible	hygienic	bacteria	radiator
perishable	cupboard	surplus	quantity

1 **From the list, choose *four* liquids that are poisonous if swallowed. Add to these to make a list of liquids that should be kept out of reach of young children. What should you do if these liquids are swallowed?**

____

____

2 **Choose the appropriate form of a list word to complete the following:**

Never use a ______________ near water, as you can be ______________.

Keep sharp ______________ in a special place to avoid accidents.

Always use ______________ on cuts and abrasions to avoid infection.

Avoid ______________ of food by ______________ by keeping perishable food refrigerated.

3 **Give one word in place of each of the following phrases or words:**

recovering from illness ______________

clean or sanitary ______________

to put into use ______________

to spoil by introducing foreign matter ______________

nourishment ______________

emit rays of light or heat ______________

easily absorbed ______________

to remove ______________

to rot or to die ______________

enclosed place for storage ______________

excess ______________

amount ______________

4 **Expand these word groups to form sentences:**

under hygienic conditions ______________________________

to digest all the information ______________________________

disinfected the bandages ______________________________

electrical storm ______________________________

provide the nutrients ______________________________

the effects of radiation ______________________________

convalescent home ______________________________

radiant personality ______________________________

poisonous gases ______________________________

contamination of the milk ______________________________

5 **Prepare a class quiz on First Aid procedures.**

SPELLING UNIT 5 WORD EXCURSIONS

subsistence	nomadic	valleys	pastoral	rural
tributary	impervious	continent	atmosphere	agriculture
volcanoes	alluvial	peninsula	isthmus	dormant
urban	intensive	fertility	monsoon	estuary
artesian	deciduous	extinct		

1 Use words from the list to complete these sentences:

Many people have moved from rural areas to live in an _______________ environment.

_______________ trees provide good shade in summer, but allow sunlight to filter through in winter.

The Murrumbidgee River is a _______________ of the Murray River.

_______________ soils along river _______________ are very fertile.

Many primitive tribes practise _______________ farming.

_______________ tribes move on when pastures are depleted.

The _______________ becomes rarefied at very high altitudes.

_______________ bores are vital to the pastoral industry of Central Australia.

The water in these bores is kept underground by _______________ layers of rock.

2a Find a word that means:

★ a narrow neck of land joining two larger areas of land: _______________

★ a narrow piece of land projecting into the sea: _______________

★ the tidal mouth of a large river: _______________

★ tropical rains: _______________

b See if you can find an example of the first three.

_______________ _______________ _______________

c List three countries that receive tropical rainstorms.

_______________ _______________ _______________

d Volcanoes can be *active*, *dormant* or *extinct*. Explain the difference. Give examples.

____

____

____

____

____

e Use *dormant* and *extinct* to describe different nouns.

dormant _______________ extinct _______________

3 Match these columns:

pastoral industry	farming
nomadic tribes	industrial
subsistence	grazing
urban	herding
rural	growing food for own use

SPELLING

SPELLING UNIT 6 THIN OR FAT

pathetic	emaciated	skeleton	angular	scraggy
haggard	willowy	lanky	sylph-like	shrivelled
gaunt	scrawny	withered	slender	puny
wizened	shrunken	obese	corpulent	chubby
plump	podgy	paunch	bloated	brawny
overweight	outsize	strapping		

1 Choose, or form words, from the list to complete these sentences:

She looked __________ after the ordeal.

These fashions only suit __________ figures.

__________ by the sun, his face looked like tanned leather.

Nobody believed that such a __________ creature could have such reserves of strength.

His __________ features made him look like a scarecrow.

The victims from the concentration camps were so __________ they looked like __________.

Mannequins need to have __________ figures.

After all the worry his face was __________.

__________ after the big meal, he staggered away from the table.

His figure was so __________ that it was a wonder he managed to buy a suit to fit him.

His facial features were so __________ that he appeared to be thin, despite his __________ physique.

__________ in children is usually caused by overeating.

Overweight men are termed __________, while women are more likely to be described as __________.

Fat children are usually fondly labelled __________.

2a Give five list words that are flattering:

__________ __________ __________ __________ __________

b Now give five words that imply criticism or disapproval:

__________ __________ __________ __________ __________

3 Circle the jarring word:

shrivelled, pinched, shrunken, withered, shivered

obesity, corpulence, corporation, bulkiness, plumpness

enlarged, bleached, bloated, distended, swollen

boastful, brawny, muscular, strapping, stalwart

4 Write a description of a fat or thin person using words from the list.

____

____

____

5 Make up your own list of *happy* and *sad* words, and use them either in sentences, or to describe two different occasions.

SPELLING UNIT 7 -ANTS

gallant	reluctant	discordant	repentant
triumphant	important	elegant	hesitant
relevant	resistant	incessant	significant
abundant	fragrant	flagrant	dominant
conversant	extravagant	immigrant	remnant

1 Choose or form words from the list that mean:

dissonant, not in harmony ________________

valiant ________________

important ________________

outstanding ________________

plentiful ________________

hesitant ________________

unceasing, continuous ________________

scandalous, glaring ________________

pertinent ________________

contrite ________________

2 Use the correct forms of words from the list to complete these sentences:

________________ is frequently rewarded with a medal.

She was not ________________ with the literature on the syllabus.

________________ drumming on the roof, the rain blotted out the sound of the radio.

I cannot see that it is of any ________________.

Rust ________________ metals are used to build bridges.

Without any ________________ the boy dived to the rescue.

The ________________ of the spring flowers was overpowering.

The ________________ of the defeated army straggled into the town.

He had such a ________________ personality that no one dared to contradict him.

________________, the woman waved the winning lottery ticket.

3 Complete this table:

	Noun		Noun
hesitant	*hesitation*	significant	
reluctant		abundant	
triumphant		discordant	

4 Find, or form from the list words, antonyms for:

confident ________________

unacquainted ________________

scarcity ________________

harmonious ________________

frugal ________________

obscure ________________

5 Make these words opposite in meaning by adding prefixes:

____relevant ____significant ____important ____repentant

6 Only two of the words in the list can be used as nouns. What are they?

________________ ________________

SPELLING

SPELLING UNIT 8

DO YOU WANT TO BE A MILLIONAIRE?

wholesaler	producer	creditor	deficiency
customer	tertiary	accountant	suite
consumer	ledger	primary	debtor
calculation	deficit	furniture	profitable
taxation	executive	consignment	warehouse
secondary	delivery	detach	correspondence

1 Complete these flow charts:

primary ——→ secondary ——→ ____________

____________ ——→ wholesaler ——→ ____________

2 What is the difference between a *customer* and a *consumer*? A *suite* and a *suit*?

____

____

3 Match these columns:

A debtor is someone	their taxation to an accountant.
Money collected from taxation	should be accompanied by a delivery note.
A creditor	should be carefully filed.
Important executives like to have	is someone to whom you owe money.
Correspondence on business matters	is used by the government to pay for services like education.
A consignment of goods	who owes you money.
Many people leave the calculation of	well-furnished office suites.

4 Find words from the list that mean:

separate ____________ amount by which expenditure exceeds receipts ____________

manager ____________ a lack or insufficiency ____________

lucrative ____________ a set of bookkeeping accounts ____________

depot; store ____________ professional keeper and inspector of accounts ____________

5 Now expand these word groups to make sentences:

furnish with ______________________________

delivery to ______________________________

deficient in ______________________________

accountable to ______________________________

detach from ______________________________

profit from ______________________________

in debt to ______________________________

consigned to ______________________________

correspond with ______________________________

over-taxed his strength ______________________________

6 Use *detached* and *calculating* in sentences to describe a person's attitude.

____

____

SPELLING

SPELLING UNIT 9 -IOUS, -EOUS, -OUS WORDS

glorious laborious victorious injurious studious industrious	**BUT:**	courteous piteous spontaneous courageous outrageous	generous glamorous mountainous marvellous ridiculous villainous mischievous clamorous rigorous

1 Find synonyms from the list (-ious, -eous), for:

instinctive ________________ diligent ________________

arduous ________________ extraordinary ________________

harmful ________________ polite ________________

2 From the same list, find adjectives that could be used to describe these nouns:

________________ outfit ________________ student

________________ cry ________________ reaction

________________ remark ________________ boy

3 Fill the blanks using appropriate parts of the words listed:

The miser was certainly not renowned for his ________________.

________________, the student ploughed through his homework.

________________, the little girl taunted her elder brother.

Subjected to constant ________________ because of her handicap, the student became increasingly introspective.

________________ training schemes were devised for the Olympic athletes.

________________ swells caused the tiny yacht to capsize.

The child was punished for the ________________ way in which she spoke to the visitor.

Everyone ______________ at the intricate design of the Opera House.

People ________________ at the door of the stadium demanding the return of their money, when the pop group failed to appear.

Smoking is ________________ to your health.

Such an ________________ comment deserves censure.

4 Some of the words listed describe admirable qualities—others negative ones. Make up a *credit–debit* table, containing these words and adding as many others as you can think of:

e.g.

Credit	**Debit**
generous *spontaneous* *honest*	*grudging* *hesitant* *hypocritical*

SPELLING UNIT 10 PLAY THE GAME

amateur	professional	individual	attendance
supporter	strength	athletic	association
acclaim	contestant	challenge	circuit
weariness	attempt	circular	spectator
presentation	champion	arrangement	specialise

1 **Expand these word groups to make sentences:**

temporary arrangement: ______________________________

polished performance: ______________________________

skilled professional: ______________________________

challenging task: ______________________________

spectator sport: ______________________________

2 **Find appropriate forms of the words listed that are opposite in meaning to:**

generalise ______________ energy ______________

deride ______________ absence ______________

professional ______________ weakness ______________

3 **Complete the following sentences with the correct forms of list words:**

The reigning ______________ issued a ______________ to his opponent.

On completion of a victory ______________ of the track, the new champion waved to acknowledge the ______________ of the crowd.

Muscles are ______________ by regular exercise.

Mohammed Ali has been ______________ as one of the greatest boxers ever.

His ______________ to challenge the leading ______________ ended in failure.

4 **Complete this table:**

Verb	Adjective	Noun
attend	*attentive*	*attendance*
support		
weary		
challenge		
attempt		
challenge		

5 **See how many of the words from this unit you can include in a paragraph describing one of the following:**
The day your team won the grand final; The original Olympic Games; An outback rodeo.

____

____

____

____

____

____

SPELLING

SPELLING UNIT 11 DON'T BEAT AROUND THE BUSH

truly	principal	aghast	illumination	progress
puncture	instruction	recognition	bicycle	appointment
distribution	intrusion	amount	discussion	remuneration
invasion	number	distinguish	revenue	suspension

1 Can you spot the redundancies (words used unnecessarily) and inaccuracies of expression in these sentences? Rewrite them correctly:

Truly and really, we were aghast.

____

We are not making any forward progress.

____

The principal repeated again his instructions.

____

Carefully she opened up the parcel.

____

It was a big, huge monster.

____

Please ring up the dentist and cancel the appointment.

____

There were less students there than last year.

____

The reason why he was late was because his bicycle had a puncture.

____

He distributed the right amount of papers.

____

2 Rewrite these words, supplying prepositions that are used with them:

illuminated ______________ recognition ______________ invaded ______________
suspended ______________ distinguished ______________ discussed ______________
instructed ______________ appointment ______________ progress ______________

3 Circle the jarring word:

intrude, interrupt, trespass, infer
assault, invasion, defence, attack
illusion, enlightenment, illumination, clarification
remuneration, donation, revenue, salary
extension, discontinuation, suspension, cancellation

4 Expand these word groups to make sentences:

The unwelcome intrusion ______________________________
Belatedly recognising the cyclist, ______________________________
The distinguished guest ______________________________
The remuneration for such a big task ______________________________
Illuminated by candle-light ______________________________
Aghast at the sudden invasion of ______________________________

SPELLING

SPELLING UNIT 12 HAVE YOU A SENSE OF HUMOUR?

wealth	humility	moderately	awkwardly
scarcity	poverty	temporarily	extremely
achievement	contraction	gracefully	rigid
confusion	accidentally	boastfully	hostile
expansion	genuine	permanently	flexible

1 Match up words from Column 1 with suitable words from Column 2.

Column 1	Column 2	Column 1	Column 2
wealth	help	artificial	friendly
truth	order	courteous	notorious
scarcity	humility	rigid	cautious
conceit	poverty	famous	public
achievement	contraction	hostile	impolite
confusion	failure	restless	lazy
expansion	glut	reckless	flexible
hindrance	fiction	diligent	stable
accidentally	permanently	private	genuine
moderately	awkwardly		
temporarily	modestly		
gracefully	extremely		
boastfully	deliberately		

2 Find words from the word list to use in the spaces below:

_______________ of food

false _______________

_______________ structure

_______________ attitude

_______________ incapacitated

_______________ balancing

_______________ of metal

abject _______________

_______________ crippled

_______________ insulting

3 You are a salesperson who claims he/she can sell anything to anyone. You have a skeleton of a sheep that you wish to sell to a musician.
OR
You might like to sell some other useless item to an unlikely buyer; e.g., suntan oil to an Eskimo.
Write the argument that you would use to persuade him/her to buy it, using words from the list wherever possible. Present your argument to the class.

SPELLING

SPELLING UNIT 13 TO TEASE THE MIND

rival	boastful	shrewd	conclusion
delicate	celebrating	conference	inclined
complimented	constitution	while	memento
trophy	banquet	tiresome	metre
agreed	frequently	bickering	explained
straight			

1 Can you solve this problem after filling in the blanks with words from the list?

Two kangaroos, both i__________d to be __________, were always arguing about who was faster at jumping. As their friends found their boasting __________, they arranged a __________ to settle the matter. It was __________ that the two kangaroos would race along a st__________, marked, fifty__________ course, turn and jump back to the starting point. The larger kangaroo, whose __________ was strong, covered four metres in one jump, __________ the smaller and more de__________ one covered two metres in one jump. However, the latter jumped more __________ and managed to keep pace with his r__________l. At the __________ of the race, the winner was __________ and presented with a __________ as a m__________o of the occasion. At the b__________t c__________g the occasion, a __________ old kangaroo __________ how the race was won.

Who won? Why? (The answer is at the foot of the page.)

2 Complete this table:

Verb	Noun	Adjective
celebrate	*celebration*	*celebrated*
	conference	N/A
		frequent
	constitution	
inclined		
	conclusion	
		straight
	compliment	
explain		

3 Find synonyms from the word list for:

quarrel __________

tedious __________

souvenir __________

cunning __________

feast __________

4 What do *strait* and *complement* mean? Use them in sentences:

____

____

____

____

Solution:

The smaller kangaroo won as he landed on the turning point, whereas his rival landed beyond it. This gave the smaller kangaroo a lead on the way back.

SPELLING UNIT 14 ABANDON SHIP

predicament	saturate	exhaustion	perilous
visibility	abandoned	auxiliary	vigilance
communication	simultaneous	wreckage	impending
launch	disastrous	negligence	contemplate
circumstances	different	navigation	collapsible

1 Find a word from the list that means:

total fatigue ______________
put into operation ______________
a difficult set of circumstances ______________
wet through ______________
imminent ______________
consider ______________
contact with others ______________
secondary, support ______________
hazardous ______________
degree to which sight is possible ______________
deserted, discarded ______________
carelessness ______________
watchfulness, alertness ______________
able to be folded down ______________
at the same instant ______________
planning of direction or speed ______________
remains ______________
tragic ______________

2 Complete this table:

Verb	Adjective	Noun
navigate	*navigational*	*navigation*
exhaust		
		visibility
	abandoned	
neglect		
	different	

3 Expand these word groups to make sentences:

To contemplate such an idea ____
Negligence at any time ____
Navigational aids ____
Abandoning the search ____
Exhaustive investigation ____
Reaching saturation point ____
Prepared for the impending storm, ____

SPELLING

SPELLING UNIT 15 -ABLE WORDS

unavailable	reasonable	capable	admirable	comfortable
suitable	irritable	inflammable	innumerable	imaginable
memorable	dependable	vulnerable	impressionable	creditable
honourable	advisable	uncontrollable	agreeable	manageable
irreplaceable	noticeable	changeable	serviceable	

1 Find words listed that mean:

able to be relied upon ________________

able to burn (easily) ________________

able to manage efficiently ________________

able to be hurt, open to attack ________________

able to be influenced easily ________________

able to be controlled, handled ________________

not able to be counted ________________

able to be rational ________________

able to be seen ________________

2 Form adverbs from the list words to use with:

upset ________________

attired ________________

seated ________________

weeping ________________

3 Use *creditable* and *credible* in sentences:

____

____

4 Make these words opposite in meaning by adding prefixes:

____available

____honourable

____suitable

____reasonable

____manageable

____serviceable

____comfortable

____agreeable

____imaginable

____capable

5 Find a word from the list that could be used with the following:

silence ________________

achievement ________________

equipment ________________

expectations ________________

mistakes ________________

accommodation ________________

child ________________

occasion ________________

for comment ________________

weather ________________

position ________________

flaw ________________

materials ________________

painting ________________

hairstyle ________________

companion ________________

6 Use the correct form of each word in brackets:

Understandably, she was (irritability ________________) and (discomfort ________________) as she stood in the rain.

Unfortunately, the young child was (control ________________) when she threw temper tantrums.

I was (agreeable ________________) surprised when I saw who entered.

SPELLING

SPELLING UNIT 16 DOUBLE MEANINGS

invested	vacation	luminous	diary
insulation	conflicting	isolation	insolvent
guerilla	respectably	insoluble	respectfully
convention	gorilla	dairy	inflicting
vocation	ludicrous	invention	infested

1 Cross out the word used incorrectly and write the correct word from the list:

Necessity is the mother of convention. ______________

When the man could not pay his debts he was declared insoluble. ______________

As the battle was now lost, the general withdrew his gorillas from the jungle. ______________

The debater, determined to put forward his inflicting opinions, rose to reply to his opponent. ______________

As the dial on Peter's watch was ludicrous, he was able to tell the time in the dark. ______________

There was a large gathering present to see the governor infested in his office. ______________

He raised his hat respectably to the old lady. ______________

Paul discovered that it was his vacation to be a public servant. ______________

The boy collected several loads of manure from Jim's diary. ______________

As the novelist wanted quietness in order to write, he went into insulation. ______________

2 Rewrite these sentences, inserting list words (or forms of them) in the spaces provided, then punctuate correctly:

According to my ______________ I have an appointment on Tuesday.

The orchard which normally produces first-quality fruit is being ravaged by hairy ______________ from the jungle.

Sound ______________ costly though it is will have to be installed.

The problem although not ______________ will hold up work for some time.

3 Match up each word with its synonym:

ludicrous	holiday
vacation	overrun
damage	practice
infested	harm
convention	absurd

4 Use these phrases in sentences:

insoluble substance ______________________________

vacated premises ______________________________

money invested ______________________________

respectable citizen ______________________________

secure investment ______________________________

conventional argument ______________________________

SPELLING

SPELLING UNIT 17 THIS SPORTING LIFE

dominate	vigorous	restriction	exceptional
spectator	competitive	anticipate	forfeit
participate	authority	attainment	flagrant
sponsor	opponent	tenacity	disqualify
achievement	incentive	attitude	exemption

1 Complete these sentences using the correct forms of the list words:

Sport so often ______________ the headlines in our newspapers.

Unfortunately so many people are involved mainly in ______________ sports, without ______________ actively themselves.

Governments are beginning to ______________ fitness programs as ______________ exercise is essential for maintaining health.

The ______________ of a high degree of excellence in sport is unnecessary for enjoyment.

Inducements are frequently offered to players as an ______________ to win matches.

At school, many students believe that ______________ sport can undermine a person's self-confidence.

______________ from school sport could be granted on medical grounds.

Ball games develop the ability to ______________ an opponent's move.

______________ breaches of rules should be punished severely.

Persistent infringements should lead to ______________.

Teams that encourage violent play should be compelled to ______________ the match.

______________ skilled players should be encouraged to coach younger team members.

2 Circle the jarring word:

stubborn, tenacious, obstinate, persuasive
promise, persistence, potential, latent ability
adversary, opponent, individual, rival
sponsor, patron, saint, promoter
advantageous, helpful, competitive, beneficial
restriction, hindrance, curb, permission

3 See how many adjectives ending in *-ant* you can add to this list:

flagrant, reluctant, hesitant, gallant, discordant, relevant, ______________________________

____

____

____

____

4 Set up a class debate:
Should sport be compulsory?
OR
Competition brings out the best in an individual.

5 Write a newspaper account, in the style of football reporters, to report a skipping or a frog-jumping competition. (Use list words.)

SPELLING UNIT 18 FOR LEGAL EAGLES

detection	investigation	evidence	comprehend
notify	prosecution	confession	enforceable
witness	allegation	defendant	juror
prosecutor	acquittal	apprehend	testify
judgment	persevere	defiance	adjourn

1 Complete these sentences using appropriate forms of the words listed:

It is the responsibility of every citizen to ______________ police of any crime committed.

Exhaustive ______________ is often required to ensure the conviction of a criminal.

The police have to collect as much ______________ as possible.

______________ to the crime by the criminal makes the prosecution's job easier.

______________ are called to try to prove the ______________ against the defendant.

The barrister representing the ______________ will present testimony in his/her client's defence.

No defendant is forced to ______________.

Sometimes a case is ______________ to allow more evidence to be collected.

After a criminal has been found guilty, he/she must face ______________.

A suspect is ______________ if evidence is inconclusive.

2 Give the appropriate forms of words from the word list for:

put off, postpone ______________

discharge ______________

proof ______________

to seize, arrest ______________

discovery ______________

persist ______________

a member of the jury ______________

a person facing a charge in court ______________

able to be carried out ______________

voluntary admission of guilt ______________

decision passed by the court ______________

openly disobedient, challenging authority ______________

3 Expand these word groups to make your own sentences:

detect a crack ______________________________

falsely alleged ______________________________

witness an accident ______________________________

apprehensive of the outcome ______________________________

4 Complete this table:

Verb	Adjective	Adverb	Noun
apprehend	*apprehensive*	*apprehensively*	*apprehension*
	comprehensive		
		defiantly	
			defence

5 Use the words *prosecute*, *persecute*, and *persevere* in sentences:

____

____

____

SPELLING

SPELLING

UNIT 19 BUYING A CAR

manufacturer	vehicle	licence	insurance	manual
roadworthy	license	registration	automatic	deteriorate
scrutinise	prominent	automation	warranty	validity
defective	assurance	guarantee	endorse	authorise

1 Complete the following, using the correct forms of the words listed:

It is compulsory to:

obtain a driver's ______________.

take out third-party ______________.

display your ______________ sticker.

It is sensible to:

ensure that the dealer's ______________ is in order.

study the owner's ______________ carefully to familiarise yourself with the car.

be sure to ______________ the car to find any defects.

ensure regular servicing to maintain your vehicle in ______________ condition.

Remember:

A warranty covers only ______________ parts, so you still have to pay for labour costs.

A warranty becomes ______________ if other than an ______________ service centre carries out repairs.

If your eyesight is ______________ your licence will need to be ______________.

It is illegal to drive:

an ______________ vehicle an ______________ vehicle as an ______________ driver

2 Use *insure* and *assure* in sentences to show the difference in meaning.

____

____

3 Give synonyms from the word list for:

faulty ______________

worsen ______________

authenticity ______________

outstanding ______________

warranty ______________

study ______________

4 Expand the following word groups to make sentences:

guaranteed delivery ______________________________

manually operated ______________________________

deterioration in relations ______________________________

invalid argument ______________________________

scrutinised his face ______________________________

authoritative source ______________________________

story was manufactured ______________________________

prominent nose ______________________________

endorsed candidate ______________________________

assured future ______________________________

registered player ______________________________

SPELLING UNIT 20 -ENT WORDS

convenient	indulgent	deficient	impudent
competent	insolent	efficient	fluent
dependent	indolent	diligent	equivalent
resilient	different	incident	evident
permanent	persistent	confident	eloquent

1 Choose or form words from the list that mean:

efficient ________________

obviously ________________

able to express oneself easily and quickly ________________

able to speak smoothly and well ________________

recovering, buoyant ________________

painstaking ________________

lacking ________________

capable ________________

persevering ________________

insulting ________________

2 Find the appropriate forms of words from the list that are opposite in meaning to:

courteous ________________

similarity ________________

energetic ________________

independent ________________

3 Choose or form words from the list to complete these sentences:

Her ________________ nature enabled her to return quickly to normal after the tragedy.

________________ in French and Italian, she found travelling in Europe easy.

________________, he stretched his body on the hot sand.

The last student spoke so ________________ that she received a standing ovation.

________________, we followed the instructions.

Despite the ________________, I rearranged my schedule.

If children are ________________ too much, they become precocious.

After ________________ questioning, the culprit finally confessed.

Her health suffered because of a mineral ________________ in her diet.

Lacking in ________________, she found it very difficult to enter the conversation.

That is hardly ________________ to the amount you borrowed from me.

4 Make these words opposite in meaning by adding a prefix:

____convenient ____dependent ____competent ____efficiency

5 What does the word *indifferent* mean? Use it in a sentence.

____

____

6 Expand these phrases to make sentences of your own:

Under different circumstances ________________

Impudently, she ________________

Indulgently, the parents watched as ________________

Permanently stationed at ________________

Evidently confused, ________________

Competently tackling ________________

SPELLING

SPELLING UNIT 21 A WEIGHTY PROBLEM

dictionary	pivot	packaged	pollute
wrapped	logically	therefore	corrupt
weighing	assembly	defile	challenge
anxious	tease	applied	wholly
determination	balance	contaminate	resolved
determined			

1 Fill in the blanks with words from the list:

While screws were being p__________d and __________ on an __________ line, a mistake was made in one of the last eight boxes filled. As the foreman did not wish to open the eight boxes, he __________ to find the light box by w__________g. He only had a simple __________, which consisted of two pans hung from a beam centred on a p__________t. As the bell to finish work had sounded, the foreman was __________ to discover the light box as quickly as possible. He t__________re __________ his mind __________ to the problem and quickly arrived at a solution. In only two weighings he found the light box.

How did he do it? (Solution below.)

2 Supply the missing words from the list:

To solve the problem above, you need to think __________.

Solving a problem is a __________.

Difficult problems __________ the mind until they are solved.

The student needs __________ if he wants to solve a tricky problem.

Use a __________ to find the meaning of difficult words.

3 Find four words in the list that have similar meanings to *taint*. Use each in a sentence.

____

____

____

____

4 Complete these sentences:

Without John as pivot in our team, __________

Facing the court on a charge of bribery and corruption, __________

We assembled all __________

Watching the trapeze act with great anxiety, __________

Confronted by weighty problems, __________

__________ was a challenging task.

To ensure a balanced diet, you __________

Wholly maintained by his parents, __________

Solution:

He weighed three packets in each pan. If these balanced, only one more weighing would be needed. If they did not, he would put aside the three heavy ones, place one of the light ones in each pan and keep one in his hand. He would then have the solution.

Spelling Unit 22 Shh ...

potential	substantial	torrential	confidential
influential	initial	preferential	beneficial
artificial	controversial	resolution	organisation
assertion	connection	contradiction	civilisation
distinction	concession	procession	recognition

The 'sh' sound in the middle of a word is rarely spelt that way, unless a root word is changed by adding a suffix (e.g., astonishment). Exceptions are cushion, fashion, bushel.

1 Which of the listed adjectives would describe:

issue ______________ downpour ______________

reaction ______________ treatment ______________

danger ______________

2 Match these phrases with nouns from the list:

______________ of terms ______________ of the problem

______________ in the ancient world ______________ for his handicap

______________ of his rights ______________ between the two meanings

3 Complete this table:

Verb	Adjective	Noun
assert	*assertive*	*assertion*
contradict		
recognise		
initiate		
confide		
prefer		
benefit		
distinguish		
concede		

4 Complete these sentence fragments:

Potentially, it is ______________________________

Her artificial smile ______________________________

Despite the controversy ______________________________

Resenting the preferential treatment given to the recruit, the older players ______________

____

So contradictory were his statements, ______________________________

No concession will be allowed ______________________________

In recognition of his contribution ______________________________

Whispering confidentially, ______________________________

There was substantial proof ______________________________

Resolutely he strode ______________________________

Following the principal's assertion ______________________________

____

SPELLING

SPELLING UNIT 23 UNITY IS STRENGTH

diagrammatic	ugliness	quest	expedite
neutrality	guarantor	portion	propulsion
impeccable	rigid	nastily	peculiarity
regrettable	formally	tries	reality
reputable	remember	reversal	possesses

SPELLING

1 Using list words, complete these sentences:

_______________ is an adjective from *diagram*.
A _______________ is one who gives a *guarantee*.
_______________ means *faultless*.
_______________ is the adverb from *nasty*.
_______________, don't forget, is spelt with *emem*.
_______________ is a noun from *peculiar*.
_______________ is an adjective from *regret*.
_______________ is the 3rd person singular of *possess*.
_______________ is the opposite of *beauty*.
_______________ is the adverb from *formal*.
_______________ is a noun from *realistic*.
_______________ is a noun from *propel*.
_______________ means *search*.
_______________ is an antonym for *flexible*.
_______________ is a noun from *reverse*.
_______________ is a verb from *expedition*.
_______________ means *part*.
_______________ is a noun from *neutral*.
_______________ is the 3rd person singular of *try*.
_______________ is an adjective from *reputation*.

2 Complete each of these sentence fragments:

During the concert, a regrettable incident _______________
Neutral countries _______________
Although the firm is reputable, _______________
As guarantor for the loan, _______________
Peculiar circumstances _______________
In remembrance of the scientist's services to mankind _______________

3 Find appropriate forms of words from the list meaning:

to hasten the progress of _______________
odd _______________
to drive forward _______________
faultlessly _______________
unfortunately _______________
not committed to either side _______________
stiff, stately _______________
search _______________
drawing, illustration _______________

4 Working in pairs, make up your own divided sentences using *ten* words from previous units. Ask your friends to join them.

SPELLING UNIT 24 CARS

maintenance	faulty	minority	overhaul
mechanical	aggressive	automobile	suspension
competence	confidence	divergence	decisive
defensive	consequence	belligerent	frustrating
unscrupulous	excessive	concerted	compulsory
reputable	justification	concentration	velocity

1 Copy and complete with the appropriate forms of the list words:

Remember: The wearing of seat belts is ________ in most states.

Careful ________ is essential to ensure the vehicle is kept in roadworthy condition.

Any ________ faults should be promptly repaired.

Vehicles should be regularly ________ to detect faults in the s________n.

Sustained ________ is vital while driving.

It is difficult to justify ________ speed.

There is no ________ for ________ behaviour at the wheel of a car.

When ________ from a lane of traffic, clearly indicate your intention.

Be ________ when making decisions, as hesitation can have disastrous ________.

A ________ driving course will increase your confidence and ________.

All governments are making a ________ effort to reduce the road toll.

2 From the list, find synonyms for:

speed ________

car ________

deviation ________

belligerent ________

respectable ________

proficient ________

and antonyms for:

satisfying ________

majority ________

insufficient ________

perfect ________

3 Expand these word groups to make sentences of your own:

scrupulous attention to detail: ________

divergent tracks: ________

minority groups: ________

justifiable behaviour: ________

compulsorily acquired: ________

reputable company: ________

velocity of the plane: ________

competent performance: ________

aggressive manner: ________

defensive answer: ________

4 See how many of the list words you can use to write out advice for a prospective buyer of a space ship, a tractor or a motor bike.

SPELLING UNIT 25 ONCE BITTEN, TWICE SHY

prescribed	infancy	prosecuted	vacate	veteran
vaccinate	literacy	hysterical	instinct	infantry
lunacy	explanation	anecdote	persecuted	veterinarian
antidote	historical	extinct	proscribed	historic
exclamation				

1 Circle the word(s) used incorrectly and write the correct word from the list:

Certain books are proscribed for study in the English course in order to improve the lunacy of the students. ______________ ______________

When my cat was sick, I took it to the veteran. ______________

The general sent his best infancy divisions to ward off the attack. ______________

If fire breaks out, vaccinate your premises immediately. ______________

The moment when the British flag was planted at Port Jackson was hysterical. ______________

When the boy did not have his homework completed, the teacher asked him for an exclamation. ______________

If we continue to use insecticides at our present rate, birds will become instinct. ______________

After listening to the colonel's boring story, James decided to relate his own antidote. ______________

2a Match these columns:

veteran	books
hysterical	mark
prescribed	reaction
instinctive	patient
exclamation	athlete

b Now use each pair of words in a sentence.

____

____

____

____

____

3 Fill in the blanks with words from the list:

Although in ______________ children seem less likely to catch serious diseases, it would be ______________ to take them to cholera-infested areas without bothering to ______________ them.

4 Write sentences using these phrases:

lunatic scheme: ______________________________

rampant hysteria: ______________________________

witness for the prosecution: ______________________________

historical fact: ______________________________

SPELLING

Spelling Unit 26 Redundancies and Inaccuracies

reiterate	recapitulate	embarrassment	verbal
tongue	veteran	recognition	regardless
literally	potential	symptoms	recurring
professional	visibly	disappear	diminutive
unanimous	essential	bronchial	alternative
alternate	forcibly		

A redundant word is one that expresses something that has already been said.

1 Circle the redundancies:

Let me reiterate again.

Perhaps I should recapitulate back to what I said previously.

Embarrassed, the boy stood still while the teacher gave him a verbal tongue lashing.

An old veteran like that deserves recognition.

The boy has much future potential.

The symptoms appear to be recurring again.

Greg Chappell is a paid professional.

I saw the cake visibly disappear before my eyes.

She was such a tiny little diminutive creature.

We all agreed unanimously.

I am going to forcibly compel him to complete the task.

It is most essential that we submit the case to the committee.

2 How often have you heard these mistakes or meaningless phrases? Correct them:

I am going irregardless of the weather. ____________________

I was literally up to my ears in mud. ____________________

The patient had an infection in his bronical tubes. ____________________

Previously we have visited our relatives on alternative Sundays. ____________________

Each and every one of us here must have heard these mistakes. ____________________

____

3 Use these phrases in sentences of your own:

relative to: ____________________

unanimously decided: ____________________

recapitulation of the argument: ____________________

alternatively, we should: ____________________

regardless of the consequences: ____________________

professional status: ____________________

potentially disastrous: ____________________

inflammation of the bronchial tubes ____________________

symptomatic of the disease: ____________________

to reiterate: ____________________

recurrent problem: ____________________

if we accept the literal translation: ____________________

SPELLING

SPELLING UNIT 27 CONFUSING WORDS

elicit	persistent	incredulous	ingenuous
illicit	consistent	incredible	ingenious
moral	notable	dependant	immigrate
morale	notorious	dependent	emigrate
illusion	allusion	proficient	efficient

1 Match a word from the list with each phrase:

unable to do without something, someone ____________

cleverly contrived, clever at inventing ____________

extract ____________

artless, innocent ____________

competent, capable ____________

confidence ____________

reference to ____________

one who is reliant on another ____________

not too ready to believe ____________

uniform, regular ____________

unbelievable ____________

adept, practised ____________

illegal, forbidden ____________

deception, delusion ____________

commonly known, infamous ____________

ethical, virtuous ____________

important, famous ____________

persevering ____________

2 Complete these sentences with the appropriate forms of list words:

He was so ____________ on his surfboard that he could perform ____________ tricks.

The new motor was so simple yet so ____________ that everyone wondered why such a system had not been invented before.

He was under no ____________ as to what was meant.

The ____________ of the team was low following their defeat.

The ____________ to the incident embarrassed her.

She was so ____________ in her attitude, it was difficult to believe she would lie.

Dismissing my story with an ____________ sneer, she walked out.

The ____________ export of native birds from Australia is heavily penalised.

Young children are ____________ on their parents.

Having captured the ____________ criminal, the police were commended for their work.

To ensure publicity, all the ____________ art critics were invited to the exhibition.

____________ as it sounded, the story was true.

____________ questioning by the police ____________ the information necessary to convict the suspect.

Few people want to ____________ from Australia.

Taxpayers can claim deductions for their ____________.

3 Use these words in sentences to show that you understand their meanings:

proficient: ____

efficient: ____

immigration: ____

emigration: ____

persistent: ____

consistent: ____

SPELLING

SPELLING UNIT 28 WORD MAZE

queasy	pursued	inflection	accede	literacy
apprehend	affectation	industrious	respectable	query
perused	respectful	incustrial	literary	comprehend
exceed	infliction	persistent	affection	consistent

1 Replace the words in italics with correct words from the list:

As John was a very *industrial* boy, we were not surprised when he won first prize in the science competition. ______________

As the coffin passed, the mourners kept a *respectable* silence. ______________

I would like to *exceed* to your request, but I cannot justify the expense. ______________

The foreign language teacher sometimes used the wrong *infliction* when speaking. ______________

The teacher threatened to exclude the *consistent* talker from her lessons. ______________

The policeman *perused* the robber across the fields, hoping to *comprehend* him. ______________ ______________

The *affectation* Joan felt for her father showed on her face. ______________

I felt very *query* after eating a large quantity of rich food. ______________

As the professor had read and written many books, he was regarded as a *literacy* man. ______________

2a Match these words:

respectable	revolution
literate	insurance
troublesome	argument
industrial	infliction
consistent	citizen
comprehensive	population

b Use each pair in a sentence:

____

____

____

____

____

3 Complete the table:

Verb	Adjective	Adverb	Noun
respect	*respectful*	*respectfully*	*respect*
exceed			
	apprehensive		
		persistently	
	querulous		

4 What does respective mean?

____

SPELLING

Spelling Unit 29 Verbal Roundabout

dismissal	cafeteria	minister	back-bencher
possibility	mayor	isolate	recommendation
overwhelmed	self-indulgent	resolute	interview
survive	tragedy	disclosed	distressing
demonstration	majority	committee	opportunity
estimated			

1 Insert suitable words from the list in each sentence:

The ______________, Alderman Gruffy, ______________ that the money spent on improving parks and gardens was approximately twenty-five million dollars.

If you ever have the misfortune of being caught in a violent street ______________, escape at your earliest ______________.

The vast ______________ of the city workers are still travelling long distances to work as a result of the bridge damage.

The formation of a ______________ to investigate the ______________ of the Energy Commission is of prime importance.

The new ______________ is being built at such a distance from the offices of the ______________ and back-benchers that there is a distinct ______________ that it will run at a loss.

2 Expand these word groups to make sentences:

an overwhelming desire: ______________________________

majority rules: ______________________________

a distressing situation: ______________________________

self-indulgent thoughts: ______________________________

follow her recommendation: ______________________________

survive at all cost: ______________________________

estimate the degree of: ______________________________

a distinct possibility: ______________________________

leading to the dismissal of: ______________________________

3 Go around the class: one person chooses or forms an adjective from words in the list; the next person has to give a suitable noun to use with it; the third person uses the phrase in a sentence. For variation, take nouns and form adjectives.

SPELLING

SPELLING UNIT 30 PROS AND CONS

argument	summarise	condemn	opponent
subside	defeat	relevant	contribution
piercing	refuting	graciously	rebuttal
criticise	reasonable	logically	significant
misinterpret	outrageous	emphasise	intonation
digress	querulous	monotonous	modulated

1 Complete each sentence using words from the list to fill the blank spaces:

How well do you argue in a debate?

When ____________ your opponent, did you c____________n him or ____________ his ____________?

Did you use pauses to ____________ s____________t points in your speech?

Was all your information r____________t or did you ____________?

Did you ____________ your argument at the end?

Did you shout down your o____________t in your ____________ of his argument?

Did you vary ____________ or was your speech ____________?

Did you deliberately m____________t your opponent's remarks?

Was your voice well m____________d or did it become ____________?

Did you accept d____________ g____________?

Did you pause to allow laughter to ____________?

Was your speech r____________e or did you make ____________ claims?

Was your argument presented ____________?

Was your ____________ to the team effort worthy?

2 Complete this table:

Verb	Adjective	Noun
criticise	*critical*	*criticism*
	significant	
summarise		
digress		
condemn		
		argument
		contribution

3 Use each of these words in a phrase:

condemnation: ____________

contribute: ____________

pierce: ____________

refutation: ____________

logical: ____________

misinterpretation: ____________

outrage: ____________

emphatic: ____________

querulous: ____________

SPELLING

SPELLING UNIT 31 NEAR ENOUGH IS NOT GOOD ENOUGH

collusion	spectre	guerilla	suspicious	infernal
resolve	internal	sceptre	reservation	septic
recitation	prospective	sceptic	perspective	angel
collision	angle	revolve	griller	superstitious

1 Circle the word used incorrectly and write the correct form of the word from the list:

The two cars met in a head-on collusion. ____________

The young man was dreading the interview with his perspective employer. ____________

As the boxer was suspicious, he rubbed his rabbit's foot before the fight. ____________

At the barbeque, the hostess fried the steak on a guerilla. ____________

If you ask my advice, you will soon revolve your problem. ____________

The boy could not solve his Mathematics problem because he did not realise the angels in the triangle were equal. ____________

The Minister for Infernal Revenue explained that the country was in the grip of inflation. ____________

The Red Indians who broke the law were confined to the recitation on their release from prison. ____________

One of the signs of royal office is the spectre. ____________

As the man did not believe the scientist in spite of all the evidence, he was regarded as a septic. ____________

2 Fill in the blanks with forms of words from the list:

As the money was stolen during morning break, the teacher was ____________ of all those seen in the room at that time.

The earth ____________ around the sun.

Little did the spy realise that his partner, who appeared so trustworthy, was in ____________ with his enemies.

Try to place the problem in ____________.

He ____________ to put his plan into action.

3 Match these words:

spectre	hellish (abominable)
resolution	sharp
reserved	conspiracy
infernal	apparition
collusion	cynical
angular	determination
sceptical	virtuous
angelic	reticent

4 Use these words in sentences to show other meanings they have:

reservation, resolve.

____

____

SPELLING

SPELLING UNIT 32 CAREERS

translator	researcher	scriptwriter	beachcomber
courier	proprietor	technician	philosopher
supervisor	unionist	lieutenant	colonel
consultant	bursar	commissioner	secretary
autobiographer	janitor	locksmith	saxophonist

1 Write one word from the list for:

a person who spends his life on beaches, not earning any money, but living as a layabout _______________

a person who is skilful in a particular field _______________

a person who writes her own life story _______________

an overseer; one who controls and directs work _______________

an owner _______________

a person who belongs to a trade union _______________

a person who transports the goods of others for a fee _______________

a specialist who is approached for advice _______________

a person who seeks the meaning of knowledge and existence _______________

a person who holds office because he was appointed by a commission _______________

a person who translates books from one language to another _______________

a person who looks after the correspondence and arranges the appointments of her employer _______________

a caretaker of a building _______________

a person who makes locks _______________

a person who plays the saxophone _______________

a person who tries to discover new facts by critical scientific study _______________

a person who is treasurer of a college _______________

a person who writes the dialogue for films _______________

2 For each phrase, form an adjective from the word in italics to qualify the noun.

technician: _______________ data

supervisor: _______________ capacity

autobiography: _______________ novel

philosopher: _______________ treatise

secretary: _______________ position

researcher: _______________ grant

3 Choose *five* people from the list. Writing one sentence for each person, explain why you would (or would not) like to have his/her position.

SPELLING

SPELLING UNIT 33 TEACHER'S PET (HATES)

environment	scraping	recommend	remember
conscious	criticism	parallel	separate
rhythm	rhyme	temporary	surprise
coming	medicine	alcohol	scrapped
embarrass	possession	accommodation	existence
necessity	government	definite	loneliness
mischievous	vehicle	parliament	interruption
February	schedule	theory	refrigerator

1 Find words from the list that match the words and phrases:

timetable ______________

aware ______________

disapproval ______________

rasping ______________

need ______________

belittle ______________

isolation ______________

naughty ______________

supposition ______________

lines that never meet are ______________

opposite of permanent ______________

a break in the continuity ______________

surrounding conditions ______________

month following January ______________

unexpected occurrence ______________

approaching ______________

suggest ______________

disconnected ______________

life ______________

absolute ______________

beat ______________

recollect ______________

ownership ______________

living quarters ______________

seat of government ______________

used to treat illness ______________

removed from use ______________

carriage or conveyance ______________

repetition of sound ______________

ruling body ______________

intoxicant present in beer, wine, etc. ______________

cabinet designed for cold storage ______________

2 Provide words, or forms of words, from the list that could be used with these words or phrases:

______________ conditions

constructive ______________

______________ to the coast

______________ stupor

swaying to the ______________

______________ by the suggestion

______________ of terms

______________ of his error

______________ the sheep from the goats

______________ for mercy

______________ incapacitated

______________ is nine-tenths of the law

it is not ______________ correct

______________ prank

SPELLING

SPELLING UNIT 34 TWENTY QUESTIONS

Choose a word circle. Working in pairs, make up a list of twenty questions based on the activities used in the units, for example:

- ★ **Spell the word ____________**
- ★ **Give a synonym/antonym for ____________**
- ★ **Form a descriptive word from ____________, etc.**

Use your questions to test the rest of your class:

foundation assertion
demonstration justification
exhibition convention civilisation
association imitation realisation
reflection ignition expedition
recognition edition
definition superstition

angrily guiltily
easily hungrily centrally
gaily sleepily eerily warily
stealthily skilfully basically
completely really truly frantically
comically tragically hurriedly publicly
generally occasionally practically
courageously gradually obviously
evidently awkwardly
periodically

past
passed moral
morale chose choose
uninterested disinterested
principal principle imminent
eminent picture alternative
pitcher alternate personnel
illegible personal eligible
bought brought

available
reasonable
capable admirable
comfortable suitable
irritable inflammable
innumerable imaginable
memorable dependable
vulnerable impressionable
creditable honourable
advisable uncontrollable
manageable irreplaceable
noticeable changeable
serviceable
agreeable

repentant
triumphant relevant
incessant abundant reluctant
tolerant resultant flagrant
immigrant hesitant repentant
significant valiant arrogant
consultant occupant
defendant remnant

quarrelled
tunnelled controlled
travelled worshipped
permitted admitted
committed forgotten forbidden
enrolled repelled propelled
compelled cancelled
transferred referred
deferred concurred
conferred occurred
recurred

potential
substantial torrential
confidential initial influential
preferential partial beneficial
artificial controversial
commercial

SPELLING

Comprehension Comprehens

Comprehension

AMANDA FORD AND ELIZABETH HAYWOOD

This section is designed to help consolidate comprehension skills in the context of enjoyable, contemporary material. Within seventeen double-page units a wide range of material is presented, including extracts from novels and magazines, poems, newspaper articles and instructional material. The emphasis is on providing different styles and genres of writing in order to develop a detailed understanding of written material. Questions are grouped according to accepted approaches to reading comprehension:

- What is being said? (literal comprehension)
- What does it mean? (inferential or interpretive comprehension)
- What do I think about it? (evaluative or implied comprehension)

Responses will consist of both short answers and more sustained pieces of writing, of which the longer pieces will be done off the page. Writing to be completed off the page is indicated by the icon.

The opportunity for extension is provided in the 'What do I think about it?' section of each unit. Questions should generally be answered in complete sentences.

n Comprehension Comprehen

COMPREHENSION UNIT 1 BOY

Papa and Mama

My father, Harald Dahl, was a Norwegian who came from a small town near Oslo, called Sarpsborg. His own father, my grandfather, was a fairly prosperous merchant who owned a store in Sarpsborg and traded in just about everything from cheese to chicken-wire.

I am writing these words in 1984, but this grandfather of mine was born, believe it or not, in 1820, shortly after Wellington had defeated Napoleon at Waterloo. If my grandfather had been alive today he would have been one hundred and sixty-four years old. My father would have been one hundred and twenty-one. Both my father and my grandfather were late starters so far as children were concerned.

When my father was fourteen, which is still more than one hundred years ago, he was up on the roof of the family house replacing some loose tiles when he slipped and fell. He broke his left arm below the elbow. Somebody ran to fetch the doctor, and half an hour later this gentleman made a majestic and drunken arrival in his horse-drawn buggy. He was so drunk that he mistook the fractured elbow for a dislocated shoulder.

'We'll soon put this back into place!' he cried out, and two men were called off the street to help with the pulling. They were instructed to hold my father by the waist while the doctor grabbed him by the wrist of the broken arm and shouted, 'Pull men, pull! Pull as hard as you can!'

The pain must have been excruciating. The victim screamed, and his mother, who was watching the performance in horror, shouted 'Stop!' But by then the pullers had done so much damage that a splinter of bone was sticking out through the skin of the forearm.

This was in 1877 and orthopaedic surgery was not what it is today. So they simply amputated the arm at the elbow, and for the rest of his life my father had to manage with one arm. Fortunately, it was the left arm that he lost and gradually, over the years, he taught himself to do more or less anything he wanted with just the four fingers and thumb of his right hand. He could tie a shoelace as quickly as you or me, and for cutting up the food on his plate, he sharpened the bottom edge of a fork so that it served as both knife and fork all in one. He kept his ingenious instrument in a slim leather case and carried it in his pocket wherever he went. The loss of an arm, he used to say, caused him only one serious inconvenience. He found it impossible to cut the top off a boiled egg.

from *Boy* by Roald Dahl

COMPREHENSION

What is being said?

1 Definitions: what is the meaning of the following?

prosperous ______

majestic ______

fractured ______

dislocated ______

excruciating ______

orthopaedic ______

ingenious ______

2 Where did Roald Dahl's father come from? ______

______

3 When was Roald Dahl's grandfather born? ______

______

4 If his grandfather had been alive in 1984, when Dahl wrote *Boy*, how old would he have been? ______________________________

5 What did his grandfather do for a living? ______________________________

6 What important event had happened just before his grandfather's birth? ______________________________

7 How did Dahl's father come to break his left arm? ______________________________

8 Why did the doctor mistake the fractured elbow for a fractured shoulder? ______________________________

9 What steps did the doctor take to treat the injury? ______________________________

10 What was the end result of the doctor's mistake? ______________________________

11 What difficult things could Dahl's father still manage to do for himself with only one arm, four fingers and a thumb? ______________________________

12 What is the only thing he couldn't manage to do? ______________________________

What does it mean?

13 What does Dahl hope to explain by telling us that his father and grandfather were 'late starters so far as children were concerned'? ______________________________

14 What important changes have occurred between 1870 and now in the practice of medicine, as shown in this extract? ______________________________

15 What does Harald Dahl's approach to life after the amputation tell us about him? Identify at least two qualities which he shows and provide evidence of each one? ______________________________

COMPREHENSION

What do I think about it?

16 If you were writing your autobiography where would you start? (It might be with your parents or grandparents, or with a notable event in your childhood. It doesn't necessarily have to be with your birth.)

17 Describe your worst childhood accident. What were you doing? How did it happen? How did you feel? How was it treated? How did other people react? Were there any lasting effects?

18 Describe a colourful character in your family.

COMPREHENSION UNIT 2 WEATHER

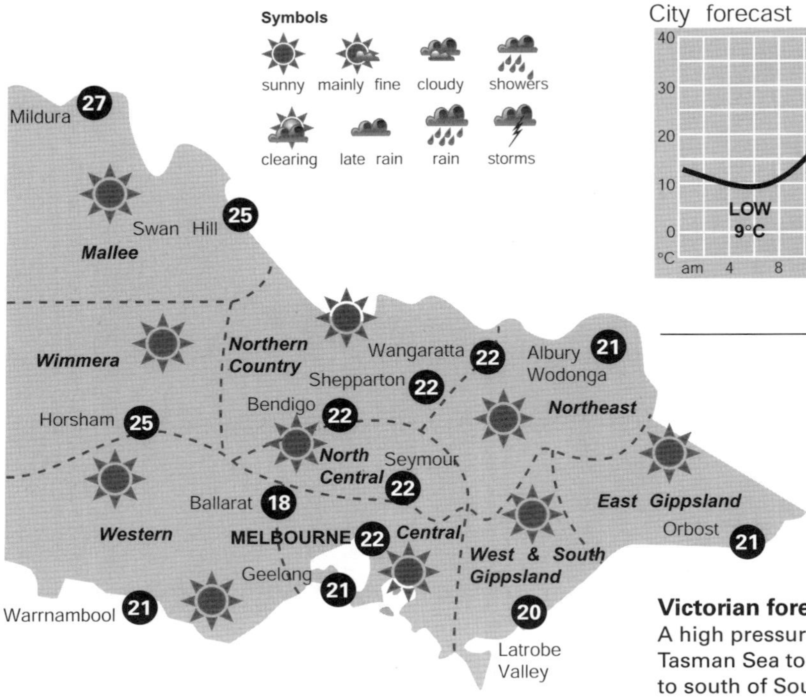

City forecast

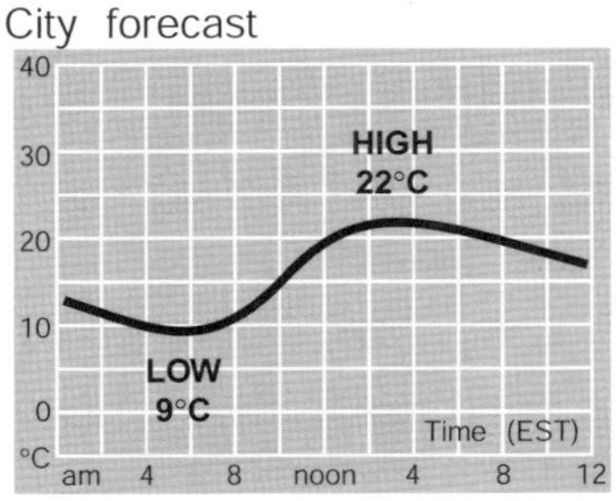

City Outlook

Tomorrow: Max 26
Fine. Mainly sunny.

Thursday: Max 18
Shower or two.

Friday: Max 22
Fine. Mainly sunny.

Trend for Saturday, Sunday and Monday:
Mainly fine. Warm at first then becoming cooler.

The Bays

Variable winds at 5–10 knots shifting N/NE at around 15 knots during the morning. Afternoon sea breezes to 10 knots. Waves increasing to around 1 metre.

Victorian forecast

A high pressure system will move eastwards over the Tasman Sea today and Wednesday. A cold front will move to south of South Australia on Wednesday then through Victoria on Wednesday night and Thursday. Another high pressure system will rapidly develop behind this front and move to the Tasman Sea during Friday.
Fine apart from morning fog in the east. Early frosts inland. A mild to warm and sunny day with light wind tending moderate northerly in the west. Afternoon coastal sea breeze.

Snow report
www.vicsnowreport.com.au or phone 1902 240 523 (55c/min)

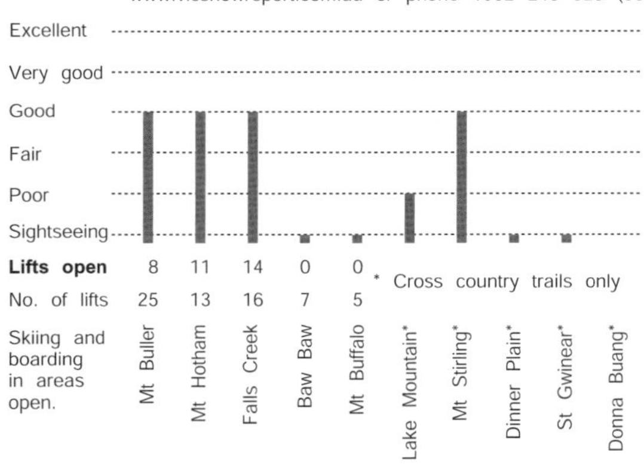

EPA Air Quality index
For update www.epa.vic/gov.au

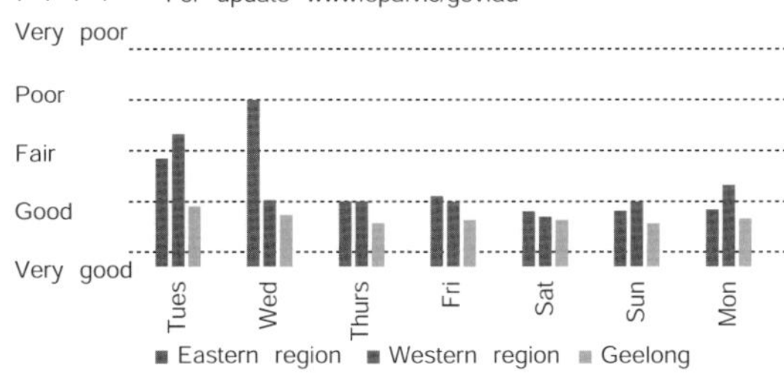

What is being said?

1 Definitions: what is the meaning of the following?

tending ____________________

moderate ____________________

isolated ____________________

variable ____________________

knots ____________________

2 Which Victorian city should expect the lowest temperature? ____________________

____

3 Which Victorian city should expect the highest temperature? ____________________

____

4 What temperature should Melbourne expect? ______

5 At what time, approximately, will Melbourne reach its forecast top temperature?

6 At what time, approximately, will Melbourne experience its lowest temperature for the day? ______

7 What sea will the high pressure system move over? ______

8 What is the estimated top wind speed for the Bays? ______

9 Approximately how high will the waves on the Bays become? ______

10 What is the address for the EPA (Environment Protection Authority) website? ______

11 How many lifts are open at Falls Creek? ______

12 What is the worst rating that can be given for air quality? ______

13 What is the best rating that can be given for snow conditions? ______

14 What is the trend for the weekend? ______

What does it mean?

15 Will I need to take a warm coat to work on Wednesday? ______

16 Should I take an umbrella to work on Thursday? ______

17 Would Saturday or Sunday be a better day to hold a barbecue? ______

18 Would the snow be better at Mt Buller or Falls Creek? ______

19 On which day, and where, will the air quality be worst? ______

What do I think about it?

20 Weather forecasters (meteorologists) are often criticised for getting the weather forecast wrong. Design a poster praising their work.

COMPREHENSION

THE SILVER FOX

Suddenly, something caught Emily's eye. A slight movement among the overgrown shrubs. She stared at the place where the foliage had trembled briefly. Something was down there. It must be an animal of some sort, but it had only been visible for a second and she hadn't been able to decide what it was.

But she *had* been able to see that it was no ordinary animal.

She leant out of the window as far as she dared and kept very still, waiting to see if the strange creature would appear again. For a long time she stayed there, tense and alert. But nothing happened. Everything was quiet and still.

Emily stretched and rubbed her eyes. Maybe I imagined it, she thought, and turned to go back to bed. But just as she started to move away, she saw it again.

She hadn't imagined it then! There was definitely something there. Something moving stealthily through the bushes.

The sky was getting lighter now and Emily could see more clearly. It was certainly an animal, but what could it be? Emily frowned as she watched it trot quietly across the garden, the light catching its sleek fur. And then suddenly she realised …

'It's a fox!' she whispered to herself. She looked again and, even though the light was still dim, she could see that it wasn't an ordinary fox with russet-coloured fur.

Its fur was silver. A bright, sleek, shining silver.

Then, as quickly as it had appeared, it vanished again. Emily couldn't say where it had gone. One moment it was there, in the garden below her, and the next it had slunk away, noiselessly.

Emily let out her breath. 'A silver fox!' she murmured.

And then, suddenly, the feeling of wonder was overtaken by something else. She was gripped by an acute, unreasonable fear, a sense of foreboding, as though the fox was some sort of warning, a warning that something dreadful was going to happen.

From *The Silver Fox* by Rosemary Hayes

What is being said?

1 Definitions: what is the meaning of the following?

shrub ______

foliage ______

alert ______

stealthy ______

sleek ______

russet ______

foreboding ______

2 What first caught Emily's eye? ______

______

3 What did Emily think was causing the movement in the shrubs? ______

______

4 What did Emily see when she leant out of the window? ______________________

____

5 Why did she turn to go back to bed? ______________________

____

6 What did she see as she started to move away from the window? ______________________

____

____

7 What helped Emily to see more clearly? ______________________

____

8 What did Emily realise she was looking at? ______________________

____

9 What colour is the fur of an ordinary fox? ______________________

____

10 What was the colour of the fur of the fox Emily saw? ______________________

____

11 What feeling replaces Emily's feeling of wonder? ______________________

____

12 Why does Emily feel fear? ______________________

____

What does it mean?

13 Why might Emily have thought that what she glimpsed was no ordinary animal? ______

____

____

____

____

14 Why did Emily stretch and rub her eyes? ______________________

____

____

What do I think about it?

15 What sort of warning do you think the fox might represent?

16 What do you think might have happened in this book? Write an outline for the rest of the story. (At least 100 words)

HAWAIIAN MONK SEAL

The Hawaiian monk seal, so named for the cowl-like fold of skin at its neck and for its solitary habits, exists only in Hawaii. The Hawaiian name for the animal is *ilio holo kai*, meaning 'the dog that runs in the sea'.

This species has remained nearly unchanged for 15 million years, though in the past century it has been in danger of dying out completely. Fortunately, conservation efforts, including the translocation of some seals to create a better male–female ratio, appear to be bringing the seals back from the edge of extinction. The Hawaiian monk seal population has risen about 15% in the past decade to a total of approximately 1300 seals.

Hawaiian monk seals, which are sensitive to human disruption, breed and give birth primarily in the Northwestern Hawaiian Islands. In recent years, however, sightings of monk seals hauling themselves onto beaches on the main islands—primarily in Kauai, but also on the northern shores of Oahu, Maui and Molokai—have increased.

The annual birth rate for the monk seal pups is between 150 and 175 a year, though because of shark attacks and other predators, the majority fail to reach maturity. Monk seals feed on reef fish, eels, octopus and lobster.

Of the world's two other monk seal species, the Caribbean monk seal is extinct and the Mediterranean monk seal numbers only in the hundreds.

From *Hawaii, edition 5*
by Lonely Planet Publications

What is being said?

1 Definitions: what is the meaning of the following?

monk ____________________

cowl ____________________

solitary ____________________

conservation ____________________

translocation ____________________

decade ____________________

disruption ____________________

predators ____________________

2 Why is the Hawaiian monk seal so named? (Two reasons) ____________________

3 Where is the Hawaiian monk seal found? ____________________

4 What is *ilio holo kai*? ____________________

5 What is the English translation of *ilio holo kai*? ____________________

6 How long has the Hawaiian monk seal species remained unchanged?

7 How have translocation efforts helped bring the monk seal back from extinction?

8 How has the Hawaiian monk seal population changed in the past 10 years?

9 Where do the seals breed and give birth?

10 Where have the sightings of the seals increased?

11 How many monk seal pups are born each year?

12 Why do the majority of pups fail to reach maturity?

13 What do the monk seals feed on?

14 What has happened to the other two monk seal species?

What does it mean?

15 Why might the Hawaiians call the monk seal 'the dog that runs in the sea'?

16 Hawaiian monk seals are sensitive to human disruption. How might this affect the numbers of seals?

17 Why is it so important to preserve the Hawaiian monk seal?

What do I think about it?

18 Why do you think it is important to save species from extinction? (About 100 words)

The Conquistadors

Hernando Cortez was the first of the conquistadors. After hearing that there was gold in Mexico, he sailed from the Spanish colony of Cuba in 1519. He burned his boats on the beach at Veracruz, to show his soldiers there could be no turning back. Then he marched inland to the capital of the Aztec civilization.

A Welcome for a God

He was helped by an astonishing coincidence. The Aztecs believed that their god Quetzalcoatl was due to arrive in Mexico from the Atlantic that very year. The arrival of strange white-skinned warriors, riding horses, firing their brass cannons (none of which had even been seen or heard of before) terrified them into the belief that Cortez was their returning god.

When the Aztec king, Montezuma, allowed the Spaniards into the city, they put him in chains. Montezuma tried to keep the peace, but was killed by his own people in an uprising. Cortez had to fight his way out of the city. In a single night he lost 450 of his own men and 4000 of the Indian allies. But just over a year later he stormed back into Tenochtitlan to destroy the city, and the Aztec civilization with it.

The story of Francisco Pizarro is very similar. After hearing of the gold and silver to be found in the land of Peru, he determined to conquer its people, the Incas. He slaughtered 10,000 of them and took their king prisoner, promising to spare his life if he filled a room with gold. The king did so. Pizarro then had him strangled. Afterwards he conquered the Peruvian capital with little difficulty, and went on to conquer and colonize the whole country.

Cruel Heroes

Neither Cortez nor Pizarro, nor the conquistadors who followed them and destroyed ancient civilisations all over central America, were conquerers only. They were inspired by Catholic zeal to convert the heathen and colonize new lands for Spain. They explored and mapped and built cities in their new domains, and added to knowledge of geography and science. They were regarded at the time as romantic adventurers and heroes. Today, (despite their extraordinary courage, imagination, and energy) we find their ruthlessness revolting, but people are entitled to be judged by the standards of their own times. Sad to say, Columbus and da Gama were also capable of dreadful cruelty, and so were later arrivals on the continent of America.

From *Exploration in History* by Sheila Robertson

What does it mean?

1 Definitions: what is the meaning of the following?

conquistadors ______

colony ______

Aztec ______

______

warriors ______

uprising ______

allies ______

conquer ______

slaughtered ______

Catholic ______

zeal ______

convert ______

heathen ______

domains ______

romantic ______

ruthlessness ______

COMPREHENSION

2 Who was the first of the conquistadors? ______

3 Of which country was Cuba a colony? ______

4 What made Cortez decide to set sail for Mexico? ______

5 Of which ancient civilisation was Mexico the capital? ______

6 Who did the Aztecs believe Cortez was? ______

7 What was the name of the Aztec king? ______

8 How many men did Cortez lose in a single night after fighting his way out of the city? ______

9 What happened one year later? ______

10 Which people did Francisco Pizarro conquer? ______

11 In which country did they live? ______

12 Why did Pizarro wish to conquer the Incas? ______

What does it mean?

13 Why did the Aztecs believe Cortez was Quetzalcoatl? ______

14 What was the impact of the conquistadors' journeys on the people of South America? ______

15 Were the conquistadors' motives entirely selfish and greedy? ______

16 What good, if any, came from their journeys? ______

What do I think about it?

17 What kind of men do you think the conquistadors were? Use at least one example from the extract to support your answer.

18 Imagine you were a young Aztec boy or girl when Cortez first arrived in Mexico. Many years later, you are telling your grandchildren the story. Include information about the Aztec civilisation, the arrival of Cortez, the battles and what life has been like for you since his victory. (About 150 words)

Far over the misty mountains

This is the song the dwarves sing to Bilbo Baggins in *The Hobbit*

Far over the misty mountains cold
To dungeons deep and caverns old
We must away ere break of day
To seek the pale enchanted gold.

The dwarves of yore made mighty spells,
While hammers fell like ringing bells
In places deep, where dark thing sleep,
In hollow halls beneath the fells.

For ancient king and elvish lord
There many a gleaming golden hoard
They shaped and wrought, and light they caught
To hide in gems on hilt of sword.

On silver necklaces they strung
The flowering stars, on crowns they hung
The dragon-fire, in twisted wire
They meshed the light of moon and sun.

Far over the misty mountains cold
To dungeons deep and caverns old
We must away, ere break of day,
To claim our long-forgotten gold.

Goblets they carved there for themselves
And harps of gold; where no man delves
There lay they long, and many a song
Was sung unheard by men or elves.

The pines were roaring on the height,
The winds were moaning in the night.
The fire was red, it flaming spread;
The trees like torches blazed with light.

The bells were ringing in the dale
And men looked up with faces pale;
The dragon's ire more fierce than fire
Laid low their towers and houses frail.

The mountains smoked beneath the moon;
The dwarves, they heard the tramp of doom.
They fled their hall to dying fall
Beneath his feet, beneath the moon.

Far over the misty mountains grim
To dungeons deep and caverns dim
We must away, ere break of day,
To win our harps and gold from him!

From *The Hobbit* by J. R. R. Tolkien

What is being said?

1 Definitions: what is the meaning of the following?

dungeon ______

cavern ______

ere ______

yore ______

fells ______

hoard ______

wrought ______

hilt ______

goblets ______

delves ______

ire ______

2 What do you notice about the pattern of the rhyme in each stanza (verse)? ______________

3 Why are the dwarves going 'far over the misty mountains'? ______________

4 What is the 'pale enchanted gold'? ______________

5 Describe some of the enchanted hoard of treasure in detail. (At least three items.)

6 Where did the dwarves of yore live? ______________

7 Who did the dwarves make the treasure for? ______________

8 What did the dwarves make for themselves? ______________

9 Why were the dwarves' songs unheard by men or elves? ______________

10 Why were the bells 'ringing in the dale'? ______________

11 Describe the destruction caused by the dragon. ______________

12 What happened to the dwarves' treasure? ______________

What does it mean?

13 How have the words in the first stanza been changed in stanzas five and ten? Why?

14 Why do you think dragons are usually depicted as terrifying, fire-breathing creatures who are out to destroy their innocent victims? ______________

What do I think about it?

15 Which stanza did you like the best? Give at least two reasons.

16 Copy out your favourite stanza and illustrate it.

COMPREHENSION

COMPREHENSION UNIT 7 AUSTRALIA'S INTRODUCED PLANTS AND ANIMALS

Why do introduced species become pests?

Certain animals and plants have been found in Australia for thousands, perhaps millions, of years. Over such lengths of time these animals and plants have evolved ways of surviving in Australian conditions. Species introduced to Australia have evolved to survive in their native countries, where conditions are different from those in Australia. Why is it then that so many of these arrivals to Australia's shores have been able to take over from native species?

Few predators and diseases

Many introduced plants become serious weeds in Australia simply because the insects that would eat their leaves or burrow into their stems are not found in Australia. Many diseases that affect these plants, and the diseases that affect introduced animals, are also not found in Australia. An example is prickly pear. To control this weed, the cactoblastis moth was released in Australia in 1925. The insect's larvae burrow through the plant so they collapse and die. Prickly pear was soon under control.

Disturbance helps introduced species

You may notice on a drive through a forest that many weeds grow alongside the road, while further back in the forest there are few or no weeds. Wherever the ground has been disturbed—building sites and cleared land, for example—introduced weeds are likely to be found.

In these places the natural conditions have been changed, and introduced plants have a chance of out-competing native plants. In particular, European plants are quick to invade disturbed areas. These plants have evolved to cope with disturbance.

It is a similar story for many exotic animals. Rabbits, for example, have not been able to thrive in Australia's forests. However, where the land is cleared they have found the conditions attractive and have thrived.

Introduced species have special features

Many exotic plants are capable of growing quickly and producing millions of seeds. They may have spiny stems and poisonous leaves that protect them from attack. These features help these plants to thrive and spread.

Many exotic animals, such as the cane toad, can breed quickly, producing millions of eggs or many young.

Vacancies

Some biologists believe that exotic species do well in Australia because there is a vacant niche or place for them. This is a space in the ecosystem that no other animal, or plant, has taken up. For example, there are no large native grazing animals in Australia's far north, so water buffaloes were able to move in and thrive without disturbance.

From *Introduced Plants and Animals* by Greg Pyers

What is being said?

1 Definitions: what is the meaning of the following?

evolved ______

native ______

predator ______

larvae ______

introduced weeds ______

______

thrive ______

exotic plants ______

niche ______

ecosystem ______

______

2 What is the key question in the first paragraph? ______

3 Why have many introduced species become serious weeds in Australia? ______

4 How was prickly pear controlled in Australia in 1925? ______

5 Why are introduced weeds likely to be found where the ground has been disturbed?

______

6 Why have rabbits done so well in land that has been cleared? ______

7 List three features of exotic plants that have helped them to spread. ______

8 What is the cane toad's main advantage? ______

9 How might a niche (space) in the ecosystem help exotic species? ______

10 Give an example of an exotic animal that has filled a niche in Australia. ______

What does it mean?

11 What do you think are the reasons (purposes) for writing a piece like this? Give two possible purposes. ______

What do I think about it?

15 Write a letter to a newspaper making suggestions about how to reduce the number of introduced weeds in bush areas. This could include ways of getting rid of them and ways of preventing new outbreaks. (About 150 words)

COMPREHENSION UNIT 8 SCAM

My name is Just, short for Justine. I'm not as short as I used to be, because I grew five centimetres over the Christmas holidays. I also turned fourteen and a half. Uncle gave me a half-birthday present, to cheer me up after my friend Brett went back to Sydney.

Brett and I missed each other but we could handle that. We weren't sure how Uncle and Brett's parents would handle the phone bills, though. I didn't want Uncle to stop me from ringing Brett every day, so I tried to phone while he was working.

My uncle writes crime novels about this tough private eye called Jake Hackett. He can't concentrate properly, unless he shuts his door and his window, stuffs a draught-stopper along the bottom of the door and sticks foam plugs in his ears. When our neighbour Phil Macy's kitchen exploded last year, Uncle didn't hear a thing.

(About the explosion—Phil reckons that secret agents blew his kitchen up, because he told the truth about them in his TV program, *Men in Suits*. But Kara, who's Phil's wife and Brett's sister, reckons that Phil must've left the gas on.)

Anyway, when I got home from school on Friday, Uncle's study door was still shut. I said, 'Yes!' and headed straight for the downstairs phone. Before I could dial Brett's number, I heard voices.

A deep voice growling, 'Are you Sam Wedgwood?'

Uncle's voice going, 'Hang on, I just have to pull my ear plug out ... Yep, got it. Hello, Sam Wedgwood speaking.'

I should've hung the phone up then. But I didn't. For some reason, that growly voice really scared me. I grabbed an apple from the fruit bowl, sat down on the kitchen stool and listened.

'I read about you in the newspaper,' the growler said. 'They reckon you're planning to write a true crime book about Bob Hobson, the Wombat Valley farmer who disappeared late last year. Is that right?'

From *Scam* by Jenny Pausacker

COMPREHENSION

What is being said?

1 Definitions: what is the meaning of the following?
private eye ______
draught-stopper ______
______

2 What is the narrator's name? ______

3 Why was the narrator feeling a bit sad? ______
______

4 How did the narrator avoid her uncle stopping her from ringing her friend in Sydney?
______

5 What is her uncle's name? ______

6 What does he do for a living? ______

7 What happened to their neighbour's kitchen? ______

8 What was his explanation for this event? ______
______

9 What was the name of the neighbour's TV program? ___

10 What happened when Justine got home from school on Friday afternoon? ___

11 What is Sam Shepherd's next plan for a book? ___

12 Why didn't Justine's uncle hear the explosion in Phil Macy's kitchen? ___

What does it mean?

13 Why would Phil Macy prefer to tell people that secret agents blew up the kitchen? ___

14 Why do you think that Justine couldn't hang up? ___

15 What impression of Justine do you gain from this extract? Give reasons for your answer.

16 What kind of man does her uncle seem to be? Provide evidence from the extract to support your opinion. ___

What do I think about it?

17 Imagine that you have listened in on a conversation and heard something that you wish you hadn't. Describe what happens. (About 150 words)

18 'They reckon you're planning to write a true crime book about Bob Hobson, the Wombat Valley farmer who disappeared last year. Is that right?' Continue the story from this point. (About 100 words)

COMPREHENSION

GOING DOWN LIKE LEAD

Going down like lead

Little Dipper had not been well for some time. Normally he was a livewire, his tail never stopping its frenetic wagging.

The only thing that seemed to slow him was the hypnotic glare of disdain our clinic cat would cast him from her perch on the front counter.

That was until his latest visit when he just rested forlornly in his young owner's arms.

The main problem was recurrent diarrhoea and lethargy, but his owners thought he also may be going blind.

Not what one would expect from a previously fit young terrier.

By the time we saw him his condition had deteriorated to the extent that he was vomiting, wouldn't eat and was in abdominal discomfort.

The mix of symptoms was certainly odd. It was possible that he had some form of abdominal disease, but why the blindness.

On the other hand, if he'd eaten something poisonous, one would have expected him to be better or dead by now! It had been well over a month since the symptoms began.

All this guessing could only take the diagnosis so far. This was a case that needed additional information.

This came from two sources: a more detailed history of events that led to the visit and some routine blood work.

The blood tests showed most parameters to be normal, except for a few inconsistencies in the blood cells.

The history revealed that his owners were renovating a miner's cottage and Dipper had access to all kinds of building materials, new and old.

Now it takes a leap of faith and some experience to connect the two and realise he may well have been poisoned after all.

Not by one of the more obvious quick-acting poisons, but by lead, a heavy metal that tends to be slow and insidious.

Lead poisoning is rare but does occur when dogs have access to items such as old pipes, sinkers, old paint and car batteries.

They actually like the taste and will lick or even swallow the object in question.

Fortunately, there is a specific test for lead in the blood.

Once that was confirmed, the treatment, though laborious, was fairly simple and removal of all offending items will prevent recurrence.

With a few days in hospital, Dipper was feeling much better and by the end of the week he was able to go home.

Which pleased both our cat and his master, who was still getting his head around the fact that heavy metal music somehow poisoned his dog.

By Dr Richard Lawrence

What is being said?

1 Definitions: what is the meaning of the following?

frenetic ____________________

hypnotic ____________________

disdain ____________________

forlornly ____________________

livewire ____________________

recurrent ____________________

lethargy ____________________

deteriorated ____________________

abdominal ____________________

parameters ____________________

insidious ____________________

laborious ____________________

2 How did little Dipper behave before his recent illness? ____________________

____

3 What were the main problems that his owners described? ______

4 What did they think might be happening to Dipper? ______

5 What were Dipper's symptoms by the time the vet saw him? ______

6 What other information did the vet need to help him work out (diagnose) what was wrong with the little dog? ______

7 What did the blood tests reveal? ______

8 What activity was Dipper's family currently involved in? ______

9 How is lead poisoning different from other poisoning? ______

10 How was Dipper treated for lead poisoning? ______

What does it mean?

11 Why are dogs at risk from lead poisoning? ______

12 Why did the vet start to think about poisoning when Dipper's owners described his problems as diarrhoea and lethargy, and said that he seemed to be going blind? ______

13 What made him think that it probably wasn't poisoning? ______

14 What is the joke (or pun) in the title? ______

What do I think about it?

15 Drawing on your own knowledge and the information in this article, design a leaflet that advises owners about the dangers of poisoning for dogs and the steps they should take to make their pet's environment safe.

16 The vet twice mentions 'the clinic cat'. Write an account from the cat's point of view which describes a typical day at the clinic. Read the article again to gain some information about the cat. (About 150 words)

First the cattle, now for the brumbies

If cattle grazing is closely associated with Australia's enduring Man from Snowy River heritage, then the wild brumby must surely be inseparable. Chasing wild horses made the Man a household name, but for the sake of the alpine environment, their days might well be numbered.

With the cattle grazing ban in the Alpine National Park passing through State Parliament on Friday, the focus is turning to the wild horses, deer and goats that also roam the high country.

Research into their numbers and ecological impact is scant, but ecologists agree that, like the cattle, they are taking a toll.

Parks Victoria's chief ranger for the alps, Peter Jacobs, estimates Victoria has 800–1000 brumbies in its high country; the 2003 fires and the following harsh winter are thought to have more than halved the 2002 population of about 2500.

But with the capacity to increase numbers by 25 per cent a year in favourable conditions, they could bounce back.

Most wild horses are found in the east, beyond Omeo up to the NSW border, and with the research focus having been on cattle, Parks Victoria is only now beginning to monitor brumby numbers and the effect the horses are having.

Mr Jacobs said brumbies and cattle generally do not share the same areas, but have a similar impact: bare ground where they congregate, fouling waterways, damaging bogs and moss beds and creating trails in erosion-prone country.

'They are not the type of animal the environment has evolved under — the soils and plants are not used to these impacts,' he said.

Unlike cattle, the horses are wild so can't be simply rounded up and moved. They are also more problematic because, even more so than cows, brumbies are widely perceived as integral to Australian folklore and somehow 'native' to the high country.

Poisoning or shooting would not be tolerated, as the NSW National Parks and Wildlife Service discovered five years ago when 600 horses were slaughtered by aerial sharpshooters. Public outrage ended plans to cull another 2000.

That leaves brumby-running by volunteers on horseback as the only management option.

Parks Victoria contracted the Alpine Brumby Management Association to remove 100 wild horses from the park last summer at a cost of $25 000, and Mr Jacobs expects a higher target next season. Any brumbies caught are either broken in for riding or sent to the knackery.

Mr Jacobs said numbers and impact would be monitored over the next three years to stop horses spreading and determine a manageable population size. The work will include community education on the horses' environmental impact. 'We will work with the community on their expectations for keeping the brumbies, so we can judge how we manage the horses,' he said. 'The last thing we want to do is be at odds with what the community wants. It is a balance.'

Sambar deer present a similar management conundrum. Dr Mark Burgman, an environmental science professor at Melbourne University, said the species was solitary and made making population estimates difficult.

Recent modelling suggests 100 000 and 200 000 Sambar deer were living in the high country, mainly in wet gullies and forested areas.

Sambar deer, an Indian species, are large, heavy, hard-hoofed and have a healthy appetite. Hunters are the main source of information, with anecdotal evidence that deer numbers are rising, potentially approaching critical mass.

The immediate impact they are having is localised, so the ecosystem will recover, but if the population rises significantly—which is likely—then there will be problems, according to Professor Burgman.

'They can make a mess, but for now this impact, while observable, is not appreciable. That could change in two to three years' time.'

Parks Victoria has so far relied on hunting to keep numbers in check, but is in a double legal bind. It is required to remove introduced animals, but also ensure that deer, as a registered game animal, survive in sufficient numbers for hunting.

Goats, mainly found in drier country in the far east towards the Snowy River, are another little-studied feral animal causing concern.

But perhaps the greatest long-term threat comes from people. At least 350 000 people visit the Alpine National Park every year, many looking for a wilderness experience.

La Trobe University alpine ecologist Dr Henrik Wahren says most do the right thing, but there are always some who drive through or around locked gates, or who want to make their own tracks.

'Four-wheel drives are the big political issue,' he said. 'Where they don't go is fine, but where they do go the damage is immense.'

from the *Age*

COMPREHENSION

What is being said?

1 Definitions: what is the meaning of the following?

heritage ______

inseparable ______

alpine environment ______

ecological impact ______

scant ______

ecologist ______

______

erosion-prone ______

problematic ______

integral ______

conundrum ______

anecdotal evidence ______

2 Why might the days of the wild brumby be numbered? ______

______

3 What are the three feral animals being focused on, now that cattle have been banned?

______

4 What job does Peter Jacobs hold? ______

5 Why is Parks Victoria only now starting to monitor brumby numbers? ______

______

6 List four problem areas caused by brumbies and cattle, according to Mr Jacobs.

______

______

7 Why can't brumbies simply be rounded up and moved like cattle? ______

______

8 Why do sambar deer present a management problem? ______

______

9 What is perhaps the greatest long-term threat to the Alpine Park, according to the article?

______

10 What sort of problems do people cause? ______

______

______

What does it mean?

11 What is the main point of this article? ______

______

What do I think about it?

12 Write a letter to Parks Victoria giving your suggestions for ridding the park of feral animals. Write from the point of view of one of the following:

- A bushwalker
- A hunter
- An animal lover

THE FAT MAN

Chocolate

Colin Potter was a hungry boy. His mother said he had a hole in his stomach and one day she'd get a needle and thread and sew it up. 'Ha, ha,' he said. She never let a joke go until she had hammered it to death. And her sayings, most of them to do with food, nearly drove him mad. They were like the holey tea-towels she hung on the line to dry and should have been thrown out years ago. 'Chew your food thirty-two times otherwise your stomach won't digest it,' she said. Or: 'You should wash each swallow down with Adam's ale.' Colin wanted cordial and fizz. He wanted cake and biscuits and fresh white bread and strawberry jam.

'Hard food for hard times,' she said, and gave him a crust with a smear of dripping on it. She sent him to the scullery for some Adam's ale. 'And use the same glass, don't take a new one,' she said. Fat chance, he thought. They only had four glasses—four old peanut-butter jars—and all of them were dirty already.

They were hard times. They were hungry times. Colin could remember when his father had a job and brought home two pounds ten a week and they had roasts for dinner, with gravy and baked kumara, and date roll for pudding, and a custard trifle for a treat. Now they had mince stew, and not enough of it, and curly kale, and a spoonful of mashed potato without any butter, and once a week a bread pudding to use up the crusts. Sometimes they had sago. Of all the puddings in the world, he hated sago most.

He was a skinny boy. As well as being hungry he was greedy, which got him into trouble so bad that he could have ended up in a hole down by the creek. He did end up with a broken arm, but that healed quickly. It took longer for other things to heal—but we must not get ahead of our story, which begins on the day his mother gave him bread and dripping and sent him outside. He ate it, although it was the sort of thing you fed the fowls. There was a bit of meat flavour in the dripping, from Grandma's roast of beef which they had shared last Sunday. Grandma's was the only place he got a feed these days—meat and gravy, roast potatoes, jelly and blancmange and a glass of milk. The trouble was it only happened every two or three weeks. When he went into her place after school—along the old verandah where the beer names still glowed on the windows, although Loomis was a dry town now, and down the hall past the staircase and the empty rooms to the kitchen at the back—she might give him a biscuit or a piece of cake.

From *The Fat Man* by Maurice Gee

What is being said?

1 Definitions: what is the meaning of the following?

Adam's ale ______

kumara ______

trifle ______

kale ______

sago ______

fowls ______

scullery ______

dripping ______

blancmange ______

a dry town ______

2 Why did Colin's mother say she would sew up the hole in his stomach? ______

______

______

3 What are two of the sayings she had about food? ______

______

______

4 How did Colin feel about these sayings? ______

5 What kind of food did Colin want? ______

6 What kind of food did his mother give him? ______

7 What kind of food did he eat when his father had a job? ______

8 What pudding did Colin hate the most? ______

9 What three adjectives are used to describe Colin? ______

10 When does the story begin? ______

11 Where was the only place Colin got a feed these days? ______

12 How often did he have a meal at Grandma's? ______

What does it mean?

13 What was life like for the Potter family? Give three examples to support your answer.

______

14 Why was their life like this? ______

15 When do you think this story might have been set? Give reasons for your answer. ______

16 Why do you think Colin's mother's sayings nearly drove him mad? ______

17 What do the beer names on the windows suggest that Grandma's house once was? ______

What do I think about it?

18 The extract suggests that Colin suffers more than a broken arm. The story continues: 'Colin decided to call on her [Grandma] even though it was school holidays. He started by way of Flynn's orchard ... and the swamp and the creek, but he never got there ...' Continue the story as you think it might have unfolded. (About 250 words)

19 Describe your favourite meal in detail.

20 What are the rules about food and eating in your household?

COMPREHENSION UNIT 12 CAFÉ MINIMALE

Menu

Entrée

Aromatic sweet potato soup, delicately spiced with coriander and cumin
Accompanied by crusty French bread

Simmered chicken dumplings in chilli broth
A refined broth with hearty dumplings to put some zing in your day

Plump samosas with a piquant dipping sauce

Main Course

Pan seared tuna on a bed of mashed potato, accompanied by a capsicum chutney

The ultimate hamburger—a succulent burger on a wholesome bun
Served with grilled cheese and a vibrant tomato salsa

Desserts

Our special sticky date pudding
Accompanied by fragrant cinnamon icecream and rich clotted cream

Trio of home-made icecreams—pistachio, tangerine and boysenberry
A treat your palate will relish

What is being said?

1 Definitions: what is the meaning of the following?

entrée ______

aromatic ______

coriander ______

cumin ______

simmered ______

broth ______

samosas ______

piquant ______

ultimate ______

succulent ______

wholesome ______

vibrant ______

salsa ______

fragrant ______

clotted ______

trio ______

pistachio ______

tangerine ______

boysenberry ______

palate ______

relish ______

2 Name the two spices used in the sweet potato soup. ______

3 What is served with the sweet potato soup? ______

4 The chicken dumplings have been fried. Is this true or false? ______

5 The dipping sauce served with the samosas is spicy. Is this true or false? ______

6 What is the tuna served on? ______

7 Find at least three adjectives used to describe the hamburger and its accompanying ingredients. ______

8 What flavour icecream accompanies the sticky date pudding? ______

9 How many flavoured ice-creams are served? ______

What does it mean?

10 Menus like this are fairly typical these days. Try to identify at least two features of such menus. ______

11 Reduce this menu to a much simpler one. (6–10 words for each course) ______

12 Write down the most likely words for the following spaces from the list provided: delight, accompanied, luscious, clotted, lovers, rich.

Chocolate Pudding Sublime

This ______ chocolate pudding will ______ all chocolate ______.
It is ______ by ______ vanilla icecream and ______ cream.

What do I think?

13 Design a menu cover for Café Minimale.

14 Design a new dish for the menu. It could be an entrée, a main course or a dessert.

15 What would you choose from the Café Minimale menu? Give reasons for your answer.

HOONING FUTURE FORETOLD

Hooning future foretold

Children as young as five show signs of being dangerous drivers as adults, a landmark study shows.

A future tendency to speed can also be found in children from age nine.

Signs include aggression, hyperactivity, attention problems, antisocial activities and difficulty with relationships.

The study of more than 1100 young Victorians is the first of its kind to examine links between risky driving and childhood characteristics.

The results come as alarming numbers of young drivers are getting killed and injured on Victorian roads.

According to the Transport Accident Commission, 27 per cent of drivers killed on Victorian roads last year were 18 to 25 years old, yet this age group has only 14 per cent of Victorian licences.

Australian Institute of Family Studies researcher Diana Smart said bad driving habits could start long before drivers were old enough to get behind the wheel.

'From five to eight there's an early sense that the future risky drivers were less able to stay focused or become absorbed in tasks or see things through to completion,' Ms Smart said.

'We need to help children get off to the best start they can in life. Things we can do is help them in their interactions with others and control their initial reactions.'

But she warned there was no guarantee that children who exhibited risk signs would become dangerous drivers.

The ground-breaking project has followed the same group of young people from infancy to young adulthood.

Of the 1135 Victorians now aged between 19 and 20 surveyed:

- **43 PER CENT** had crashed while driving, although most only suffered property damage;
- **ALMOST** a third had been picked up speeding by police at least once;
- **NEARLY** two thirds drove when very tired.

RACV chief behavioural scientist Anne Harris said the survey results were surprising.

'We need to be doing some broader early intervention work with young people, because for some it's too late to be getting them at 15 or 16 when they might already be on a destructive pathway,' Ms Harris said.

The report will be released today by the RACV, the Australian Institute of Family Studies and the Transport Accident Commission.

from the *Herald Sun*

What is being said?

1 Definitions: what is the meaning of the following?

hooning ____

foretold ____

landmark study ____

hyperactivity ____

antisocial ____

interaction ____

initial ____

guarantee ____

ground-breaking project ____

infancy ____

RACV ____

intervention ____

2 What does the headline 'Hooning future foretold' mean? ____

3 List five predictors of future dangerous drivers, according to the study. ____

4 What was the aim of the survey? ____

5 What percentage of drivers killed on Victorian roads last year were between 18 and 25 years old? ______

6 The 18–25 year old drivers hold ______ of Victorian licences.

7 What is Diana Smart's job? ______

8 At what age did Ms Smart find that some children were less able to stay focused?

______

9 According to Ms Smart, how can these children be helped? ______

______

10 What warning does Ms Smart give? ______

______

11 How old are the surveyed Victorians now? ______

12 List three results of the survey on these drivers. ______

______

______

______

______

13 What is Anne Harris's job? ______

______

14 What does Anne Harris suggest should be done about these results? ______

______

15 List the three groups releasing the report. ______

______

What does it mean?

16 Why might children who have difficulty focusing on tasks become dangerous drivers?

______

______

17 Why might the Australian Institute of Family Studies take an interest in this survey?

______

______

______

18 Why do you think Ms Smart issues a warning? (Question 10) ______

______

______

What do I think about it?

19 Write a letter to the editor of the newspaper giving your opinion on this survey. What is your reaction? Why?

20 Write from the point of view of ONE of the following:

- A young person about to get a driving licence
- The parent of a hyperactive child
- A representative of the Transport Accident Commission

COMPREHENSION

Hop into Hanoi

Only the traffic is a cross to bear

The wide, tree-lined avenue in downtown Hanoi is a fast-flowing stream of bicycles and motorbikes.

Step off the footpath slowly but confidently, advises a local, cross the road at a leisurely pace and do not stop.

Without slowing, the bike riders diverge slightly to the right or the left, calculating our rate of progress and missing us by centimetres.

Confidence is the key for the traveller in Vietnam. The traffic will not mow you down, the locals are friendly, the countryside is beautiful and the food is flavoursome and healthy.

Hanoi, the capital and cultural centre of Vietnam, is a stylish and gracious city that retains its old-world charm.

Visitors are often surprised to find that its French colonial heritage survived the American War, as the Vietnam War is called locally.

Much of central Hanoi is best explored by walking, particularly the Old Quarter, where narrow streets are lined with colourful shop-houses selling herbal medicines, bright fabrics, silver and jade jewellery.

A trip to Hanoi would be incomplete without visiting the father of modern Vietnam, Ho Chi Minh, whose embalmed body is on display in a huge marble mausoleum at Ba Dinh Square.

A thousand kilometres to the south is bright and brassy Ho Chi Minh City, which most people still call Saigon. Everywhere you look there is colour and movement.

Below silvery skyscrapers, schoolgirls in their traditional long white tunics chat on mobile phones. Modern shopping centres are just streets away from long-established markets and ancient pagodas.

In Cholon, Ho Chi Minh City's bustling Chinatown district, the huge, covered Binh Tay market is packed solid with merchandise.

The ground floor is devoted to food of all kinds, including tiny rose apples, lotus seeds, camomile for making tea, orange fruit used for dyeing rice, century-old eggs covered in rice husk or charcoal paste.

From the city's landmark Notre Dame Cathedral, built by the French in the 1880s, a stroll along Dong Khoi street takes you past many new boutiques and galleries as well as some of the city's best restaurants and bars.

Reunification Hall is the former Presidential Palace, home to the past three presidents. This is where tanks crashed through the gates in April 1975, an event which came to symbolise the end of the Vietnam War.

By Alan Hill,
Herald Sun

What is being said?

1 Definitions: what is the meaning of the following?

cross to bear ______

leisurely ______

diverge ______

old-world charm ______

French colonial heritage ______

______

embalmed ______

mausoleum ______

lotus shaped ______

brassy ______

pagodas ______

symbolise ______

2 What are the main forms of transport in downtown Hanoi? ______

______

3 What is the advice of a local about crossing the road? ________________________________

____

4 How is Hanoi described in the fifth paragraph? ________________________________

____

5 What often surprises visitors to Hanoi? ________________________________

____

6 What are some of the goods sold in shop-houses in the Old Quarter? ________________

____

7 What, according to this article, would complete your visit to Hanoi? ________________

____

____

8 Where is Ho Chi Minh City in relation to Hanoi? ________________________________

____

9 What was the old name for Ho Chi Minh City? ________________________________

____

10 Ho Chi Minh City is a mixture of ancient and modern. Give two examples of this mixture.

____

____

11 What five foods could you find at Binh Tay Market? ________________________________

____

12 What is a landmark of Ho Chi Minh City? ________________________________

____

13 What happened at the former Presidential Palace in April 1975? ________________

____

COMPREHENSION

What does it mean?

14 Why is the traffic the only 'cross to bear' in Hanoi, according to this article? ________

____

15 Why is walking the best way to explore the Old Quarter? ________________________

____

____

16 Compare Hanoi with Ho Chi Minh City, using information from this article. How are they different?____

____

What do I think about it?

17 Which of the two cities described appeals to you the most? Give reasons for your answer.

18 Write a travel article about a place you have visited (it could be close to home). Try to describe its appeal and the amenities available. What was the food like? (About 150 words)

YOUNG DOCTORS

Young doctors

Ever wanted to be a doctor? We talk to dedicated medical intern Helen Crowther, 24, to find out what it takes.

How did you get into medicine?

I didn't get into medicine straight from school, so I did a science degree with a double major in physiology and psychology. After that I got into the graduate medical program, which took four years. I spent time in lots of areas in medicine and did placements in the UK and India.

Why did you decide to become a doctor?

I was about seven when I decided to become a doctor. Both of my parents are nurses, so they had a big influence. I wanted to work in science and with people, so medicine seemed like the only way to do this. In Year 12 I did mainly science subjects—chemistry and physics—because I loved them and because of my career choice.

What is an internship exactly?

It's a year of supervised practice, which all graduates must do to be registered as a medical practitioner.

What does a typical day hold for you?

My day starts between 7.30 and 8.30 am. I work closely with a senior doctor, who makes most of the decisions. First, I check whether I have new patients and if anything important happened to my patients overnight. The rest of the day is mostly spent organising. Being a junior, I do most of the leg work—tests, prescribing medications and performing some procedures. I do some overtime after hours and at weekends. Unfortunately, sick people don't stick to a nine to five schedule. I'm rotated between departments—medical, surgical and emergency—every 10 weeks. At the moment I'm in the haematology department looking after patients with leukaemia and other blood-related cancers.

What are the best bits of your job?

I love working with people—doctors, nurses, patients and their families. I develop really good relationships with people who have some serious things happening in their lives. I know that I only play a very small role in this huge system, but it is very rewarding knowing that I can brighten someone's day. I work with some great staff and we always seem to have fun.

What are the worst bits?

I do a lot of paperwork—which wasn't why I wanted to be a doctor!

Do you have any advice for others interested in a medical career?

It takes a really long time to get here, and there is still a very long way to go. But I can't think of a better job if you love science and working out the reasons behind illness, working with people from all walks of life and generally being bossy! It really has been worth all the work. If you really want to do it, find out as much as possible about medicine, talk to lots of doctors … and don't listen to your maths teacher when he says you'll never make it!

By Jessica Parry,
from *Dolly*

What is being said?

1 Definitions: what is the meaning of the following?

physiology ____________________

psychology ____________________

placement ____________________

leg work ____________________

internship ____________________

haematology ____________________

2 What subjects did Helen Crowther study in her science degree? ______

3 How long did the graduate medical program take? ______

4 Where were Helen's placements? ______

5 Why did Helen decide to become a doctor (three reasons)? ______

6 Why did Helen take mainly science subjects in Year 12 (two reasons)? ______

7 Why is Helen required to do overtime after hours and at weekends? ______

8 Why is she the one who is required to do the 'leg work'? ______

9 What does she enjoy about her job? ______

10 What is her least favourite part of the job? ______

11 What is Helen's final piece of advice? ______

What does it mean?

12 Why would a doctor be required to do a lot of paperwork? ______

13 What do you think Helen is trying to suggest about her maths teacher? ______

What do I think about it?

14 Does this interview encourage you to be a doctor? Give reasons for your answer.

15 What sort of job would you like after you finish school? Explain your choice.

Old man's many moods

The Murray offers something different every day

The Murray River is unpredictable, says river captain John Jackson.

'When she's full she's quiet and beautiful,' he says, 'but in winter, when the water is low, all her snags make her quite treacherous.'

Jackson tours the ever-changing Murray near Echuca and knows this stretch of water like the back of his hand.

He steers the *Kingfisher*, a purpose-built flat-bottomed tour boat, upstream as the Murray weaves through rivergum forest.

'This is perhaps one of the most amazing parts of the Murray,' he says, 'because here the river is higher than the surrounding countryside.'

To prove the point he invites us to stand up and see for ourselves.

Our boat is higher than the floodplain and lakes around by about a metre. It's like riding on an aqueduct through the countryside.

'This is because the Murray at this point is a perched river,' he says 'Silt from floods bas built up to form natural levee banks.'

A pair of ducks pass the boat and land on Barmah Lake. This is an anabranch of the Murray that fills during floods, making it navigable for the *Kingfisher*.

For most of the year it is a shallow lake, home to a diverse range of water birds. In autumn and spring the lake is home to migratory wading birds, some from as far away as Siberia.

'Experts tell me that the lake is slowly silting up,' Jackson says.

'In 50 to 100 years, Barmah Lake will be a grassy plain with a stream running through it,' he says, inviting us to come back to see for ourselves.

Farther upstream Jackson slows the *Kingfisher* and points to an oval scar in the bark of an old gum.

'This is at least a 150-year-old scar. The Aboriginal people came along and removed the bark to make a coolamon,' Jackson says.

'That's a dish in which they'd carry mussels and yabbies. It was also used as a bed for babies.'

Jackson picks out a mighty river redgum and says it's a survivor, a tree too crooked for timber or too hollow for firewood. It could be 1000 years old.

'The river changes around the year,' Jackson says. 'At any time there's something happening.

'In winter the mist rises off the water early in the morning. In spring the migratory birds come in from all over Australia.

'At Christmas the redgums flower in profusion and after the autumn rains the native violets burst into flower.

'I've been up the river thousands of times and every time I see something different.'

Traveller's checks

Best route: Take the Hume Highway to 3 km short of Wallan, then the Northern Highway to Echuca.

Best beds: The River Gallery Inn. Rooms with spas & breakfast from $158. Ph: 5480 6902

Best meals: The Oscar W restaurant at the Port of Echuca. Ph: 5482 5133

Best thrill: The two-hour Kingfisher Wetland Cruises. Ph: 5480 1839

By Richard Cornish, *Herald Sun*

COMPREHENSION

What is being said?

1 Definitions: what is the meaning of the following?

unpredictable ____________________

treacherous ____________________

purpose-built ____________________

aquaduct ____________________

perched ____________________

silt ____________________

levee ____________________

anabranch ____________________

diverse ____________________

migratory ______

profusion ______

yabbies ______

2 What makes the Murray River quite treacherous in winter? ______

3 What is the name of Captain John Jackson's tour boat? ______

4 What body of water is an anabranch of the Murray River? ______

5 What flock to Barmah Lake in spring and autumn? ______

6 What is a coolamon? ______

7 What is the main feature of the river at Christmas? ______

8 How much would a room with a spa and breakfast at the River Gallery Inn cost? ______

9 Which Echuca restaurant is highly recommended? ______

What does it mean?

11 Why is the Murray River at Echuca higher than the surrounding countryside? ______

12 Why does Jackson believe Barmah Lake will be a grassy plain with a stream running through it in 50 to 100 years? ______

13 What does Jackson mean when he describes the old redgum as a survivor? ______

14 Who is the 'old man' referred to in the headline? Explain your answer. ______

What do I think about it?

15 Make up an interesting new headline for this article.

16 Design a poster advertising the attractions of Echuca.

COMPREHENSION

Stunt performer

Stunt performers undertake dangerous acts in order to entertain, including replacing film actors in dangerous scenes, performing with the greatest visual impact and the smallest safety risk.

Stunt performers may perform the following tasks:

- jump from high buildings
- drive cars and motorcycles at fast speeds and crash vehicles
- enter flaming buildings or set themselves on fire
- perform stunts on horses, boats, trucks and water skis
- evaluate scripts in regard to safety aspects and provide safety reports
- oversee performers on set and provide advice or assist with safety.

Stunt performers perform acts that look spectacular or appear dangerous, using timing and props to minimise risks. It takes experience and a considerable amount of time to work out a logical sequence.

Personal requirements

- quick reflexes and flexibility
- good eyesight
- a sense of timing
- responsible attitude towards safety

Education and training

There are no specific educational requirements to become a stunt performer. Training is usually given on the job by experienced staff. Employers usually prefer applicants who have finished Year 10.

Employment opportunities

Stunt performers work on contract for film companies, television stations and video production houses. They may also work in a variety of entertainment centres, including circuses, shopping centres and show grounds.

Most stunt performers start as an assistant. Extensive experience is needed to gain the necessary skills. Success is likely to depend on ability and motivation, while demand is determined by the level of investment in the television/film industry, and public interest in live performance.

AusInfo

What is being said?

1 Definitions: what is the meaning of the following?

visual impact ______

evaluate ______

props ______

minimise ______

logical sequence ______

reflexes ______

flexibility ______

extensive ______

motivation ______

2 Why, according to the job description, do stunt performers undertake dangerous acts?

______

______

3 Outline four dangerous tasks undertaken by stunt performers. ______

4 Why might stunt performers be asked to evaluate scripts? ______

5 Why would stunt performers be asked to oversee performers on set? ______

6 How do stunt performers minimise risks? ______

7 What are the personal requirements of a stunt performer? ______

8 What are the educational requirements of a stunt performer? ______

9 How are stunt performers trained? ______

10 List five possible employment opportunities for a stunt performer. ______

11 What makes a successful stunt performer? ______

What does it mean?

12 Why would stunt performers be used instead of the film actors? ______

13 Why would stunt performers want to provide the greatest visual impact? ______

14 Why do stunt performers need to spend a lot of time working out a logical sequence for stunts? ______

15 List each of the personal requirements and explain why they would be important for a stunt performer. ______

What do I think about it?

16 Describe an effective stunt you have seen on film or at an entertainment centre.

17 You are an unemployed stunt performer. Write a job application for a specific stunt job. It could be in a film or at a circus, or any entertainment venue. Make sure you sell yourself. Check the qualities required in the job description.

Writing Writing Writing Writ

Writing

AMANDA FORD AND ELIZABETH HAYWOOD

This section contains seventeen double-page units that will help develop writing skills. A variety of writing techniques is explored, such as point of view, narrative structure, vocabulary building and literary conventions. It covers a range of fiction and non-fiction text types, including informative, narrative, descriptive, instructional and persuasive, exploring forms such as biography, reports, newspaper writing, myth, fable and science fiction. The emphasis is on providing different techniques of writing, improving written expression and developing writing skills specific to particular genres.

Each unit consists of an interesting and relevant model of writing or graphic stimulus, an explanation of the technique or characteristic of the text type or genre, and space for responses. The responses will consist of both short answers and more sustained pieces of writing, of which the longer pieces will be done off the page. Writing to be completed off the page is indicated by the icon.

WRITING UNIT 1 INTRODUCTIONS

Your opening sentences are vital to making your writing interesting. They must be eye-catching and intriguing—the reader must want to read on. There are many ways to start. Here are a few examples from well-known writers:

> In fairy-tales, witches always wear silly black hats and black cloaks, and they ride on broomsticks. But this is not a fairy-tale. This is about REAL WITCHES.
>
> From *The Witches* by Roald Dahl

The reader is left wanting to know what real witches are, and why this is not a fairy-tale. The description of fairy-tale witches is vivid, too.

> 'You're not taking that dung beetle with you,' said Mum.
>
> 'But Mum, Uncle Sid likes dung beetles. He won't mind.'
>
> 'Aunt Scrotch will. She doesn't even like boys.'
>
> From the story 'Mousechap' in *Uncanny* by Paul Jennings

A dung beetle is an interesting pet. Why does Aunt Scrotch not like boys? How will this affect the story? Why is the boy going to stay with his aunt and uncle? The introduction sets up a scene that encourages the reader to continue. The use of direct speech (the actual words spoken) makes the opening more lively and immediate.

> It's only half an hour since someone—Robyn, I think—said we should write everything down, and it's only twenty-nine minutes since I got chosen.
>
> From *Tomorrow, When the War Began* by John Marsden

What needs to be written down? The writer obviously feels apprehensive about it. Who has chosen the writer? Who is Robyn? Is she the leader? Again, the reader is left wanting to find out what is going on.

1 Which sentence from each of the following pairs would make the more interesting opening for a piece of writing? Explain your choice in each case. Why is the opening you have chosen better than the other?

a I woke up at six o'clock and had breakfast.

b 'You're going to miss the bus!' screamed Belinda from the kitchen.

____

____

____

c The green slime oozed slowly under the door.

d Once upon a time there was some green slime.

____

____

____

____

e I was born in Sydney.

f Mum said I was the tiniest baby in the hospital.

____

____

____

g Sally nagged her mother until she agreed to let her go to the dance.

h 'Mum, if you let me go I promise to clean my room every week.'

i Crack! The old oak tree split in two.

j It was a dark and stormy night.

2 Make up an opening sentence for each of the following topics. You should be aiming for lively and intriguing sentences that make the reader want to continue reading.

a You discover that your mobile phone has been stolen.

b A strange message appears on your computer screen.

c The grand final (any sport)

d I nearly drowned.

e The day I crashed my bike

3 Write out three interesting introductions from a book that you have read.

WRITING UNIT 2 CONCLUSIONS

There are many ways to finish a piece of writing. You need to leave an impression on the reader. You might use a surprise ending, or you could link the ending back to the start. Whatever you choose, you should try not to resort to a common, well-known sentence (a **cliché**) such as 'They all lived happily ever after.'

Look at the ways these writers finish their stories. The openings can be found in Unit 1.

> 'You can say that again!' my grandmother cried, giving me another kiss. 'I can't wait to get started!'
>
> From *The Witches* by Roald Dahl

Roald Dahl has used direct speech to finish this book—we are also left wondering what they are going to do. We feel involved because we hear what grandmother actually says.

> In my letter back I told him the little dung beetle was doing well. I still keep it in the matchbox. But at lunch time I let it out and give it as many chocolate freckles as it wants.
>
> From the story 'Mousechap' in *Uncanny* by Paul Jennings

We learn that the boy has survived his trip and that the dung beetle has been rewarded for something. The description of the chocolates makes the reward seem special—particularly if you like chocolate freckles yourself! There is a link back to the opening of the story, as Mum has said that the boy should not take the dung beetle with him.

> Humans do such terrible things to each other that sometimes my brain cells tell me they must be evil. But my heart still isn't convinced.
>
> I just hope we can survive.
>
> From *Tomorrow, When the War Began* by John Marsden

The use of the first person ('I') encourages the reader to identify with the narrator of the story. We learn that terrible things have happened but the narrator is still optimistic that they can survive. This ending leaves the way open for a sequel—how do they survive?

1 Which sentence from each of the following pairs would make the more interesting ending for a piece of writing? Explain your choice in each case. Why is the ending you have chosen better than the other?

a We went home and went to sleep.

b 'Let's go. There's nothing else we can do to help now,' said Mike.

____

____

____

c Just as we were turning back we heard a distant roar.

d On the way back we heard a noise.

____

____

____

____

e We left the circus grounds at five o'clock and went home.

f I will never see a circus again without thinking of that fateful day.

____

____

____

2 **Make up a concluding sentence for each of the following topics. You should be aiming for lively and original sentences that somehow refer back to events in the story. Consider using short sentences or direct speech.**

a Your brother has broken your favourite game.

____

____

b You are not allowed to go to the game, but you sneak out anyway.

____

____

c My dog ran away.

____

____

d My trip to Queensland

____

____

e The worst birthday ever

____

____

3 **Using one of the ideas from exercise 2, make up an opening sentence that would fit with the conclusion you have suggested. It should provide a link to the concluding sentence.**

Topic from exercise 2: ______________________________

Your suggested opening sentence:

____

____

4 **Find several examples of interesting endings to stories or films. Discuss their effectiveness in class. Which conclusions work best? Why do these endings work better than others?**

____

____

____

____

____

____

____

____

____

____

WRITING UNIT 3 USING BETTER WORDS: SELECTION

You need to think carefully about every word you use in your writing and try to select the best word at all times. Here are some exercises to help you.

1 a Add adverbs (words that give more information about the verb) and adverbial phrases to make the writing in these sentences more vivid. Key words have been placed in brackets to get you thinking.

i The cat prowled ______________ (how) through the long grass ______________ (where) and disappeared ______________ (how) as we watched.

ii As we watched ______________ (how) the spaceship landed ______________ (where) and we gasped in amazement ______________ (why).

iii The wind howled ______________ (how) through the trees ______________ (when) and the rain drummed ______________ (where) all night long.

b Add adjectives (describing words) to add interest to the following sentences.

i The girl gave him a ______________ present.

ii The ______________ car broke down.

iii We were lost in the ______________ jungle. Great!

c Improve the sentences that follow by replacing the underlined adverbial phrases with more precise verbs ('doing' words or actions). You will not need to use the adverb when you do this.

i The boy <u>walked slowly</u> home from school.

____

ii The girl <u>spoke quietly</u> to her friend.

____

iii The woman was <u>crying loudly</u>.

____

iv The little boy <u>ran noisily</u> through the house.

____

2 Rewrite the following passage, improving it by the sensible use of pronouns (words that stand for a noun).

Mark and Omar went down to Sorrento back beach this afternoon. Omar said the waves were pretty good but Mark lost his boogie board. Mark left his boogie board on the sand when Mark went to buy Mark and Omar a drink. When Mark got back, the boogie board was gone. Mark and Omar told a lifesaver, but the lifesaver said Mark would have trouble finding the boogie board because the beach was so crowded. The lifesaver suggested that Mark and Omar look for the boogie board later in the day when the beach was less crowded.

3 **Check a piece of writing that you or a friend have done recently and try to improve it using some of the strategies that you have practised in this unit. When you have done this, write a short report, outlining the strategies you used and the changes you made.**

WRITING UNIT 4 USING BETTER WORDS: USE OF IMAGERY

In order to make your writing more interesting you should try to use images and comparisons which can bring your writing to life.

For example: 'She was a very mean woman'.

How could you describe a 'very mean' woman more effectively? Perhaps you could use a comparison, comparing her to a bitter lemon. 'She had all the sweetness of a bitter lemon.' You could also say she was 'a shrew' (a tiny aggressive mouse with sharp teeth).

Below are some examples of imagery which you can use in your own writing.

A **simile** is a comparison where on thing is said to be *like* another. The words *like* or *as* are used.

For example: 'He was as strong *as* an ox.'

The comparison here is between a strong man and an ox, which is renowned for its strength when pulling heavy loads.

1 Complete each of the following sentences with a simile of your own. Try to make up something new and original. You may use more than one word.

Example: The dog looked like a *wild mop* after it had been blow-dried.

a Helen's deb dress was as ____________________ as a ____________________.

b When she was ready to go to the deb she looked like ____________________.

c The football ground was as muddy as ____________________ after all the rain.

d I hope you are not going out looking like ____________________.

e Nathan was as angry as a ____________________ when Paul broke his TV set.

A metaphor is a figure of speech in which two things are compared by saying the first thing *is* the second thing.

For example: 'The workers feared that **heads would roll** when the new management took over.'

The workers did not fear actual decapitation—the expression 'heads will roll' refers to the loss of jobs.

2 Underline the metaphor in each of the following sentences.

a 'There's no need to snap my head off,' Mum replied angrily.

b She was about to boil over about her lost notes.

c The storm is a wild animal tonight.

d Her hair was a fluffy fantasy of fairy floss.

e She had fire in her eyes.

> **Personification** refers to a figure of speech where human characteristics are given to objects.
> For example: 'The clouds glared down on the party, ready to drop their load of rain.'
> In this example the clouds are looking down like people.

3 Write a sentence which personifies each of the following.

a A strong wind in the trees. ______________________________

____

b The sea on a calm, sunny day. ______________________________

____

4 Use any of the above figures of speech (simile, metaphor, personification) to write a sentence which describes each of the following. Try to make your images original and lively.

a A car out of control on an icy road. ______________________________

____

b An attacking shark. ______________________________

____

c An elephant bathing in the river. ______________________________

____

5 a Write a paragraph describing one of the following, using at least one simile, one metaphor and one example of personification.

- A family member (including pets)
- A wild stormy night
- Your favourite place
- Playing a game in the mud

____

____

____

____

____

____

b When you have finished, swap your paragraph with another student. Discuss the images you have both used in your descriptions. Write down the best image from your partner's writing below and explain why you thought it was effective.

____

____

____

____

____

____

____

FILM REVIEW

A **film review** should tell the reader briefly what the film is about (informative writing), but it normally includes the writer's opinion of the film as well (opinionative writing). Thus the purpose of a film review is twofold—informative and opinionative.

Here are a few points to remember when you write a film review:

- Do not give too much of the plot away, especially the ending!
- Include some brief information about the director, if possible (for example, other films made by this director).
- Include some brief information about the main actors and the characters they play. (What other films have they been in? How does this one compare?)
- Try to explain what is special about this particular film. (What makes it special? How does it fit in with other similar films? Is it better than others?)
- Give your opinion of the film with reasons and examples of incidents that back up your opinion.
- Give a final recommendation. (Who would you recommend this film to? Why?)

Here is an example of a plan for a film review.

Title of film and rating	**The Lord of the Rings: The Return of the King (M)**
Director	Peter Jackson
Brief plot outline	Based on the Tolkien fantasy, the film follows Frodo's quest to destroy the Ring with the help of the wizard Gandalf and the rest of the fellowship.
Main actors and the characters they play	Frodo (Elijah Wood) and Gandalf (Ian McKellan) play their parts superbly as usual, but it is the digitally-created Gollum who really steals the show.
What is special about this film?	Oscar-winning special effects, the spectacular New Zealand landscape and a gripping climax.
Compare with other films	The best of the trilogy.
Your opinion with reasons	Not to be missed, especially for fans of the first two films. The characters, story, action sequences and landscape all work together to provide the perfect cinema experience.
Recommendation	Anyone who loved the first two films. Lovers of fantasy and of Tolkien.

1 Read the following short review and identify the words that give the information asked for in the questions below.

***The Lord of the Rings: The Return of the King* (M)**

Everyone who has loved the previous films in Peter Jackson's fantastic and ambitious adaptation of JRR Tolkien's *The Lord of the Rings* trilogy will be bowled over by this one. It is without doubt the best film of the three. I give it four stars (excellent). I'll be returning to see it myself!

a The director's name ______________________

b The writer of the original story ______________________

c Two words that give an opinion of the film trilogy ______________________

d Who would enjoy this film? ______________________

____

e Does the writer think this is the best film of the three? ______________________

2 Write a short review (about fifty words) of a film you have seen. Your review must include: a brief comment on what the film is about; some information about the characters; your opinion; a recommendation. This exercise should encourage you to focus on the most important elements in the film, and prevent a long and unnecessary description of the plot.

Title of your film: ______________________________

Your review: ______________________________

3 Write a film review of about 250 words that includes the elements practised in the above exercises. You should be able to describe what makes the film special and give examples of incidents from the film to back up your comments.

WRITING

WRITING UNIT 6 NEWS REPORT

A **news report** must include certain information about an event or incident. It is useful to ask these questions about the incident:
- What happened?
- When and where did it happen?
- Who was involved?
- Why and how did it happen?
- What was the result?

A simple news report does not include the opinion of the writer—when opinions are given, the piece becomes **persuasive** or **opinionative**. Here is an example of a simple news report.

Headline that outlines the story

School bus over the edge

What happened? — The Smithtown College school bus ran off the road and overturned in a gully

When and where? — this morning on Beacon Hill.

Who was involved? — Seventeen students from Smithtown College were on the bus at the time.

Why and how? — The bus apparently suffered brake failure on the steep hill and failed to take a corner.

What was the result? — Luckily it came to rest on a large tree, which prevented it from rolling all the way to the bottom of the ravine. Several of the students suffered minor injuries. The bus driver is being treated for shock.

By Jason Frenkel, *Herald Sun*

1 Headlines should give some hint about the content of the report and encourage the reader to read the whole article. Make up headlines to accompany the following stories.

a A cyclone is heading for a major city.

____

b Thousands of battery hens are released from their cages at night by animal liberationists.

____

c A local youth has his mobile phone stolen as he waits for the train.

____

d The local football team wins the grand final.

____

2 Write a news report based on the following story.

A family of ducks disrupts morning traffic as it crosses the road.

Headline: ________________________________

What happened? ________________________________

____

When and where? ________________________________

____

Who was involved? ______________________________

____

Why and how? ______________________________

____

What was the result? ______________________________

____

3 Now write two news reports without the assistance of the questions. Make up your own details about each of the following stories.

a Lost child found safe and well after all-night search in the bush.

Headline: ______________________________

Report: ______________________________

b Bank hold-up in broad daylight.

Headline: ______________________________

Report: ______________________________

4 Find a news report in the paper and see if it answers the key questions: *What*? *When*? *Where*? *Who*? *Why*? *How*?

USING SIMPLE COLUMN GRAPHS

Sometimes you will need to write up the results of some research you have done. Often, after interviewing people or giving them a questionnaire, you will plot the results on a graph or chart.
There are several ways of doing this—your computer will offer some options, such as a pie chart or bar graph.

The simplest way of charting results is on a **column graph**. For example, if you asked twenty school students what they thought about reducing the school holidays, the results could look like this:

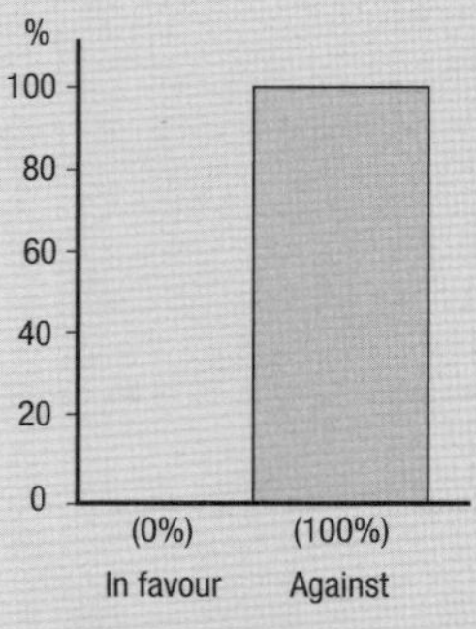

Should the school holidays be reduced?
Student responses (20 students)

If you asked twenty teachers the same question, you might get a different response:

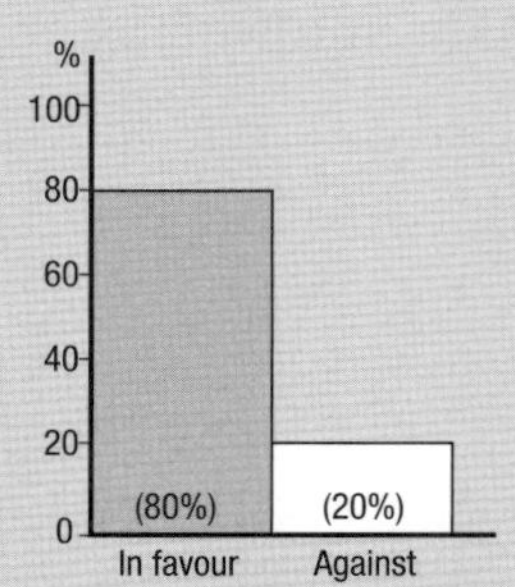

Should the school holidays be reduced?
Teacher responses (20 teachers)

It is usually necessary to interpret the results in writing. First, you could write a sentence about each of the graphs above. For example:

One hundred per cent of students were against the proposition that school holidays should be reduced.

Twenty per cent of teachers were against the proposition and 80 per cent in favour.

Next, you should interpret the results. For example:

As expected, students do not want their holidays cut. However, most teachers (80 per cent) were in favour of the proposal. Although the sample was small (only forty people in total), it seems that teachers feel they need as much class time as possible to get through the curriculum.

1 Answer the following questions about the column graphs below.

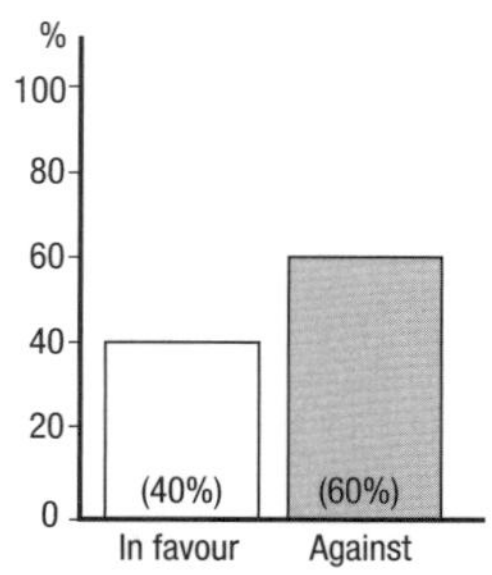

Should school uniform be compulsory?
Student responses (100 students)

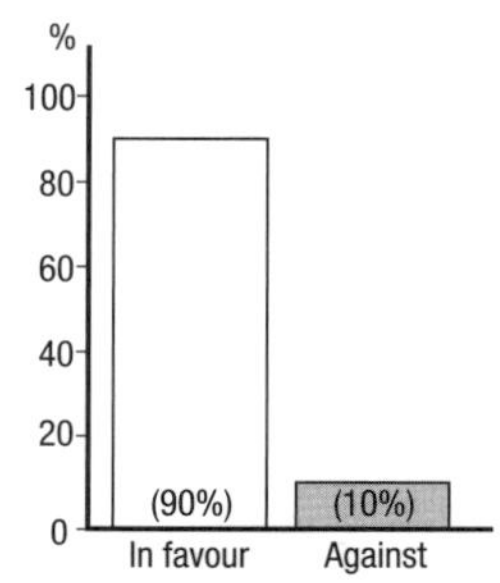

Should school uniform be compulsory?
Parent responses (100 parents)

a How many students would prefer compulsory school uniform? ______________________

b How many students would prefer not to have compulsory school uniform?

____

WRITING

c How many parents would prefer compulsory school uniform? ______________________

d How many parents would prefer not to have compulsory school uniform?

____

e What do the figures tell us about students' attitudes towards school uniform?

____

____

____

f What do the figures tell us about the parents' attitudes to school uniform?

____

____

____

g Write a few sentences interpreting these results. How would you try to explain them?

____

____

____

____

____

____

2 Conduct research on one of the following topics:

- School sport should be compulsory. Yes/No
- Computer games should be banned during the week. Yes/No
- School canteens should sell only healthy food. Yes/No

a Ask twenty classmates to respond to your topic. Write down the results. Draw a simple column graph to display the results.

b Write several sentences interpreting the results. What could they mean? Is the sample (twenty students) big enough to draw wider conclusions?

3 Make up your own topic and conduct the research. It should be a question that has a simple Yes/No answer. Ask at least twenty people. Include the following information:

a Your topic

b The results (in writing)

c Your column graph

d Your interpretation of the results.

WRITING UNIT 8

DESCRIBING A PLACE

When you are describing a place your aim is to make the scene come alive for the reader. Your task is to paint a picture with words. To do this, you need to:

- use colourful and precise adjectives (describing words)
- appeal to a range of senses (sight, hearing, smell, taste, touch)
- experiment with imagery, such as comparing one thing with another to create a more vivid picture; for example, 'In the distance the single blossom tree looked like fairy floss on a stick.'

Sometimes writers use the technique of **personification**, giving non-living things human characteristics and behaviours to give their descriptions more impact; for example, 'Tossed by the wind, the plastic bag danced across the street.'

The best descriptive writing often concludes with the writer reflecting on how the place being described makes the writer feel or what it makes him or her think about.

Here is a description of a place.

Seascape

From the cliff top on which I sat, the deep blue-green ocean stretched out before me towards the horizon, where it met with the clear sky. Below me at the foot of the towering cliffs, waves pounded against jagged rocks, sending a shower of spray into the air to be sprinkled back down like raindrops into the sea.

It made me feel peaceful. Miles of rippling waves all moving gracefully to and fro and then becoming furious and hurling themselves against the land, only to drop back and continue on their endless journey around the world.

The gentle breeze brushed my face and rustled through the straggly, dry plants which grew on top of the cliffs. Beside me, a lizard emerged from a groove in the land and scurried away to sunbake in private. Occasionally a seabird would soar with the wind high above the water, just like a kite, and then swoop down in a dive and disappear from sight. The thunder of the waves was the only sound that broke the silence. I breathed in the tangy air and felt grateful to be part of this ancient landscape—even if it was for only half an hour.

By Kim

1 **a** Which adjectives does Kim use to describe the plants on the cliff top?

____

b Provide two examples of imagery used by Kim in the first and third paragraphs.

____

____

c Provide an example of personification from the second paragraph.

____

d How does this place make Kim feel?

____

2 **Kim appeals to a number of senses in this piece. Provide an example that shows how she has appealed to each of the following:**

a Sight (first paragraph) ______________________________

____

b Touch (third paragraph) ______________________________

____

WRITING

c Sound (third paragraph) ______________________________

____

d Smell (third paragraph) ______________________________

____

3 Appealing to a range of senses, and using one example of imagery and one of personification, paint a word picture of one of the following:

- footy changing rooms after everyone has left
- a butcher's shop
- the supermarket
- a hairdressing salon
- your garden
- your bedroom
- a place that is special to you

Remember to let the reader know what the place makes you think or feel.

WRITING

WRITING UNIT 9 BIOGRAPHY

A **biography** is similar to an autobiography, with one important difference—it is written by someone else. A biography can be written about someone you have never met, such as a famous explorer from the past, or about someone you know, such as your aunt (who may be a famous singer).

Writing a biography of someone famous. If you are writing about someone famous, you should be able to find information about him or her on the Internet or in the library.

What sort of information will you be looking for?

- Place and date of birth
- Early childhood—any special events or incidents
- Schooldays—were they happy or not?
- Career—how did it start? Important events and incidents
- Any mentors? Did the person meet someone who changed his or her life?
- Try to find out what makes the person special? How would you explain this?

Writing a biography of someone you know. You will need to conduct interviews with your subject in order to find out about his or her life.

What sort of questions would you ask? The dot points above could be used as a starting point. Some people will talk for hours, in which case you will need to use a tape recorder to record all the information. Others will need prompting with specific questions; for example, 'Where were you born?'

1 You are going to write a short biography of someone you know. Start with a classmate and ask the following questions.

a Where and when were you born? ____________________

____

b Describe the members of your family. ____________________

____

____

c What sort of person do you think you are? ____________________

____

____

d Describe an interesting/happy/sad event that happened to you (for example, an injury, a special holiday, something that happened to your pet). ____________________

____

____

e What are your hopes for the future? ____________________

____

____

2 Write the first paragraph of your biography, using the information from the above responses. For example:

Melissa Jones was a lively baby. She was born on 4 May 1994 in a country hospital in Victoria. She smiled at her parents as soon as she was born. She was soon called 'Mel' by everyone except her grandmother, who thought it was a boy's name. When Mel was two years old, she won a baby contest and her mother looked forward to having a child model in the family. However, it was not to be so easy.

3 One way of structuring a biography is to use subheadings that describe different phases of your subject's life. You could use subheadings that relate to the different years of the subject's life (for example, *1990–1995, 1995–2000*), or you could use the subheadings to introduce different important events (for example, *First day at kindergarten, The day Brad lost his mobile phone, Triumphs on the basketball court*). Think about the way you might structure the biography of your subject in exercises 1 and 2 and suggest three subheadings you might use.

1 ______
2 ______
3 ______

4 Using one of your subheadings from exercise 3, compose a paragraph of about five sentences in which you give details about that time or incident. For example:

Hopes dashed

Melissa was on her way to becoming a child model—she won many baby contests and she had been crowned the cutest two-year-old at the shopping centre. One day her mother noticed that she was growing taller very quickly—in fact, she was towering over the other kids by the time she was three. She no longer won beauty competitions, but, when she was six, she took up netball and started her long and successful sports career.

5 Write a biography of an interesting person, using the information in this unit as a guide.

WRITING

WRITING UNIT 10 POINT OF VIEW: MULTIPLE NARRATIVES

You can tell a story from a number of different viewpoints and in a variety of ways. You and your parents, for example, might tell a very different story about why your school report was not as good as it could have been.

1 a Choose one of the following ideas and present both points of view.

- Why your report was disappointing. (A = parents, B = you)
- A blind date. (A = the girl, B = the boy)
- The weekend at our place. (A = you, B = the family pet)

A ______________________________

____

____

____

____

B ______________________________

____

____

____

____

b What is the advantage of this type of writing?

____

____

____

You might like to use **diary format** to tell a story. You could either tell about something that actually happened to you or you could tell an imaginative story through a series of diary entries. It is important to make your diary writing lively and interesting. Some well-known texts that are written in diary form are *So Much To Tell You* by John Marsden, *Strange Objects* by Gary Crew, *The Growing Pains of Adrian Mole* by Sue Townsend and *The Diary of Anne Frank* by Anne Frank.

2 Read Jesse's diary entries about his holiday, then list three things he could have done to make his diary entries more interesting.

Jan 2. We left home at 7.00 am and stopped in Bendigo for breakfast at McDonald's. I had a sausage-and-egg McMuffin. The trip was boring. We got to the motel in Echuca at lunchtime. It was nice. For lunch I had a salad sandwich.

Jan 3. We spent the day waterskiing. I had fish and chips for dinner.

____

____

____

____

____

____

If you are using diary entries to tell an imaginary story, aim to reveal as much as you can about the person who is writing the diary.

3 Write two diary entries by a person about their first day at a new school. One person should be friendly and happy, and the other should be shy and worried.

a ____

____

____

____

____

b ____

____

____

____

____

____

You could also write in **letter format**, where you use a series of letters between people to tell a story. You could write letters between two people where only one side is given, letters between two people where both sides are shown or a letter story that involves three or four people.

You could use business or personal letters or a mixture of both to tell your story. This type of story format works best if your letters are set over a period of at least a fortnight.

4 Write a letter story between two or more people. The events it centres around should take place over at least two weeks. Here are some ideas, or write down some of your own:

- an incident where you were in trouble at school
- a friend has borrowed something from you and has not returned it
- a neighbourhood dispute
- an apology

____

____

____

____

____

____

____

____

____

____

____

____

WRITING UNIT 11 PLOT DEVELOPMENT

Starting at the beginning and working your way through to the end (a linear structure) is only one way of telling your story. Often it is more effective to begin in the middle of the action in order to grab the reader's attention. You can then work your way back to explain how the central characters found themselves in this situation. This technique is called **flashback** and you have probably encountered it in books, films or television shows. Read the following example.

> I was in a tunnel; a dark, damp, cramped and smelly tunnel to be more precise, and the 'Who wants to be a millionaire?' question was how was I ever going to get out? There was no room to turn around, the mudslide had closed off the entrance and I didn't think I felt brave enough to keep moving forward. I couldn't believe that it was only four hours ago that I set off on my Outdoor Ed. caving excursion with such excitement. Whoever said that life can change forever in the blink of an eye sure got it right.

From this point on, the writer could explain how the character came to be in this situation and then go on to tell how everything is resolved. This is a much better start than telling the reader what the character did when the clock radio went off, what he or she had for breakfast, who he or she sat next to on the bus, and so on. Start as close as possible to the climax of your story, then fill the reader in on the necessary details later. Keep the orientation stage of your story as brief as possible.

1 Write the first paragraph of a story in which you begin as close to the climax or main action as possible and then start to explain how things came to be like this. Use a story that you have written recently or one of the following topics: The fight; Kidnapped by aliens; Lost; My most embarrassing moment.

____

____

____

____

____

____

Most writers try to build up an atmosphere of **suspense** in their stories. This is the anticipation that is created when the reader is unsure of what will happen next, and the suspense lies in the question of who or what or how. Suspense can also occur when we know what will happen but do not know when it will happen.

2 a Graph the build-up of suspense in a novel that you know well. On the horizontal axis list the beginning, the main events and the conclusion. On the vertical axis, identify three points: low, medium and high tension.

b What does your graph tell you about the build-up of suspense in your novel? What, for example, was the climax or high point for tension?

Endings are also very important, as you found out in Unit 2. You could have a surprise or 'twist' ending that is intended to take the reader by surprise or an ending where you leave some uncertainty or mystery. For example, is the evil force from space really destroyed? This can leave the reader thinking and wondering. Always avoid the anticlimax as an ending; for example, *and then I woke up, it had all been a dream*. It never works.

3 While suspense is important in all stories, it is especially important in detective stories. Write a detective story in which you include all of the following ingredients in any order you wish (you will need to make up some of your own as well): a dead body, the smell of pipe tobacco, an open window, some scraps of burnt paper in a fireplace, a missing notebook computer, a silver charm bracelet with a broken catch.

Pretend that you are the detective and tell the story.

Make sure that your orientation describes the setting, as it will probably be very important in a detective story. You will also need to introduce all the characters and outline any problems that they face. These problems will lead to the complication.

Use some techniques to make your story suspenseful. You should try to arouse the reader's curiosity but not satisfy it immediately. You could also drop some hints or clues about future events.

Start your story as close to the main action as possible and then fill the reader in on the information that he or she will need.

Try to have a twist in your ending (resolution) and tie up all the loose ends.

Your story should be about 350 words long.

WRITING

WRITING UNIT 12 GHOST STORIES

Nearly all of you will have read a ghost story or seen films about ghosts. In some of these films the ghost appears, and in some stories a description is given. In others, while the sense of the ghost is very real, it remains unseen or undescribed and sometimes these stories can be even more frightening than those in which it appears.

1 In groups or as a class, discuss examples of ghost stories that you have read or seen. After you have finished, list three things that made them scary.

a ______________________________

b ______________________________

c ______________________________

Setting is very important in ghost stories. You need to be able to create a frightening, eerie atmosphere. Unit 8 provides useful tips on how to do this.

Image

Fog covered the hills like a blanket, but not the kind of blanket that made you warm and cosy, more like one that sucked all the warmth out of your body and left you feeling chilled to the bone. Even though it was only 4.30 in the afternoon, lights started to appear in some of the houses, which were all set well back from the road. As I walked up the path to my front door, I could smell the tangy wood smoke of my neighbour's fire and I wished I was going home to a crackling fire. The leaves rustled under my feet. I felt uneasy somehow. There was a prickling sensation at the base of my spine. I fumbled for my key at the bottom of my bag and then-…

Appeals to a range of senses

Effective use of adjectives

2 Think of three good settings for a ghost story.

a ______________________________

b ______________________________

c ______________________________

Openings are also very important in ghost stories. You can have a mysterious opening with lots of atmosphere, as in the above extract, or you might choose a dramatic, sensational opening; for example, *Thud! The thunder was louder than any thunder I'd ever heard. Hang on, that's not thunder. Oh my God.* You could also try a very unusual opening that will grab the reader's attention straight away because of its oddness; for example, *The butler had one blue eye while the other was brown*. Sometimes it is best to tell the reader something about your story so that he or she will want to read on; for example, *It was very cold and uncomfortable sitting up in that attic, but Kim and Joe were determined to get to the bottom of the mystery that had been puzzling them for the last week.*

Unit 1 will give you some additional ideas.

3 **Write an exciting first line to go with each of the settings that you devised in exercise 2, then explain which kind of opening you have chosen to use.**

Setting 1: ____________________

Opening: ____________________

____

____

Type of opening: ____________________

Setting 2: ____________________

Opening: ____________________

____

____

Type of opening: ____________________

Setting 3: ____________________

Opening: ____________________

____

____

Type of opening: ____________________

4 **Write a ghost story. You can use one of the settings or openings that you have already come up with as a starting point or choose one of the following.**

Settings:

- an old pub
- a supermarket in the middle of the night
- a school

First lines:

- That first night in our new house was to turn out to be the strangest of my whole life …
- When I look back on what happened, it seems like the most horrible nightmare, but it did happen …
- 'Ghosts!' exclaimed Ky Li. 'Don't make me laugh …'
- I remember very well the night the ghost got into our house …

WRITING UNIT 13 THE BALLAD

A **ballad** is a narrative or story that is meant to be sung. In medieval times, ballads were performed by wandering musicians at fairs and in castles. Audiences used to listen, enthralled, to the dramatic stories full of daring deeds that these people told. The main characteristics of the ballad are:

- It moves quickly and directly into the story.
- It has a strong sense of rhythm and a strong rhyme that helps people remember the words.
- It often makes use of dialogue.
- It often has a refrain; that is, a group of words that are repeated.
- The story is told in a suspenseful way.
- Popular subjects are tragedy, death, adventure, the supernatural and brave deeds.
- The main emotions explored are pity, love, fear and anger.

Here is an example of a ballad.

A smuggler's song

If you wake at midnight and hear a horse's feet,
Don't go drawing back the blind, or looking in the street,
Them that asks no questions isn't told a lie.
Watch the wall, my darling, while the Gentlemen go by!
    Five and twenty ponies,
    Trotting through the dark—
    Brandy for the Parson,
    'Baccy for the Clerk;
    Laces for a lady; letters for a spy,
And watch the wall, my darling, while the Gentlemen go by!

Running round the woodlump if you chance to find
Little barrels, roped and tarred, all full of brandy-wine,
Don't you shout to come and look, nor take 'em for your play.
Put the brushwood back again,—and they'll be gone next day!

If you see the stableyard setting open wide;
If you see a tired horse lying down inside;
If your mother mends a coat cut about and tore;
If the lining's wet and warm—don't you ask no more!

If you meet King George's men, dressed in blue and red,
You be careful what you say, and mindful what is said.
If they call you 'pretty maid', and chuck you 'neath the chin,
Don't you tell where no one is, nor yet where no one's been!

Knocks and footsteps round the house—whistles after dark—
You've no call for running out till the house-dogs bark.
Trusty's here and Pincher's here, and see how dumb they lie—
They don't fret to follow when the Gentlemen go by!

If you do as you've been told, likely there's a chance,
You'll be give a dainty doll, all the way from France,
With a cap of Valenciennes, and a velvet hood—
A present from the Gentlemen, along o' being good!
    Five and twenty ponies
    Trotting through the dark—
    Brandy for the Parson
    'Baccy for the Clerk.
Them that asks no questions isn't told a lie—
Watch the wall, my darling, while the Gentlemen go by!

By Rudyard Kipling

1 a What is the subject of this poem?

b What is the refrain in this ballad?

c There is an urgent rhythm to this poem. Why might this be?

d How does the rhyme work in this ballad?

2 **To give you some practice at the ballad form, choose two of the following topics and write the first verse of each.**

- Your favourite sportsperson
- An amazing pet
- A dreadful storm
- A scary teacher

Each verse should have four lines. The first line should rhyme with the second line, and the third line should rhyme with the fourth.

3 **Write a ballad. It should have five verses and each verse should have four lines. It should tell a story in a suspenseful and dramatic way and have a strong sense of rhyme and rhythm. Try to use some dialogue in the ballad. If you are happy with it, you could type it out and provide an illustration for each verse. Various class members could also perform their ballads as travelling musicians did hundreds of years ago.**

Choose one of the following subjects:

- **your most exciting sporting victory**
- **a dramatic incident at school**
- **a brave action that you saw or heard about**
- **a famous football grand final**
- **a family outing or holiday that had a few problems.**

WRITING UNIT 14 HAIKU AND CINQUAIN POETRY

Haiku poetry comes from Japan and is used to describe nature and its beauty. The best haiku often concentrate on small-scale subjects; for example, the leaf instead of the whole tree. They are rather like close-up photographs.

Haiku are always written in the present tense. Every haiku has three separate lines and each line has a set number of **syllables**.

Line 1 always has 5 syllables.

Line 2 always has 7 syllables.

Line 3 always has 5 syllables.

A syllable is a unit of sound. The name *David* contains two syllables: *da* (1) and *vid* (1).

1 How many syllables are there in the following names?

a	Rebecca	Re/bec/ca/	____________
b	Mohammed	Mo/hamm/ed/	____________
c	Declan	Dec/lan/	____________
d	Sanjay	San/jay/	____________
e	Sam	Sam/	____________
f	Christina	Chris/ti/na/	____________
g	Your name	____________	____________

Here is an example of a haiku. The syllables have been marked off.

Rain/drops/ fall/ gent/ly/ (5)
Slow/ly/, stead/il/y/ down/ward/ (7)
Splash/ing/ all/ the/ day/ (5)

2 Mark off the syllables in the following haiku.

An old, silent pond ______________________
A frog jumps into the pond ______________________
Splash! Silence again ______________________

Write two haiku. You may choose from the ideas that follow or make up others. Remember, though, a poem about a grain of sand will probably be more successful than one about a beach.

An autumn leaf	A teardrop	Frost	A baby's finger	A summer breeze
A spider's web	A cat	Silence	A piece of driftwood	Goldfish

Remember:

Good haiku need thought
One simple statement followed
By poet's comment

a

b

Cinquain poetry has five lines. *Cinq* comes from the Latin word meaning five. Each line of a cinquain has a particular word requirement:

- Line 1 has only one word, stating the title of the poem.
- Line 2 has two words, describing the title word.
- Line 3 has three words, expressing action.
- Line 4 has four words, expressing a feeling.
- Line 5 has one word that is a synonym for the title.

A synonym is a word that is similar in meaning.

3 Rewrite the following cinquain, putting each line in its proper place.

Winter around the corner
Leaves falling, stillness
Autumn
Gentle, golden
Fall

4 Write two cinquain poems. Choose from the following ideas or make up your own.

mothers	*fathers*	*spring*	*summer*	*winter*	*teachers*
morning	*night*	*pies*	*bats*	*sharks*	

a

b

WRITING

WRITING UNIT 15 LETTERS TO THE EDITOR

Letters to the editor are written to the newspaper by members of the public. They provide a range of readers' views on issues in the news and give people the chance to reply to previously published letters. They may provide a series of letters on an issue over a number of days and they usually have a set word limit.

A letter to the editor follows the usual rules of a formal or business letter. You must include your address and the date. You write the name (The Editor) and the address of the person or organisation to which you are writing (in this case, the address of the newspaper). You then begin the letter with *Dear Sir or Madam* and end with *Yours faithfully* followed by your signature.

As a rule, these formalities are left out when the letter is printed in the newspaper, and the editor of the letters page supplies a catchy headline that sums up the writer's opinion.

As with other types of persuasive writing, skilful writers of letters to the editor use a number of techniques to make their arguments more forceful and so more convincing to the reader. These techniques include the following:

- **Emotive words.** These are words that show how the writer feels; for example, to refer to a situation as *disgraceful* is much stronger than referring to it as *unsatisfactory*.
- **Rhetorical questions.** These are questions that do not require an answer but are used to encourage the reader to agree with the writer's argument; for example, *Should we have to put up with this kind of violence on the football field?*
- **Expert opinion.** Writers often refer to experts to persuade the reader.
- **Statistics.** These are facts and figures that are sometimes used by writers to make an argument seem more difficult to disagree with.
- **Inclusive language.** The use of expressions such as, *we're tired of excuses* and *all of us realise* is designed to make the reader feel that he or she is on the same side as the writer.
- **Tone.** Another method that writers use to persuade the reader is their use of tone, or the attitude they take towards their subject and the reader; for example, the tone used might be angry, sarcastic or humorous.

The Chronicle

Lift your game, fellas!

First it was Aussie Rules footballer, Wayne Carey, and cricketer, Shane Warne. In the US we've had the outrageous behaviour of Mike Tyson and most recently claims made about basketball star, Kobe Bryant. Don't they know we're just a tiny bit sick of their antics? We've all had enough of these great big spoiled brats who seem to believe they can do whatever they please.

Child psychologist, Bill Peterson, revealed in a recent media report that violent, aggressive behaviour is on the rise in our schools. He also pointed out that sporting heroes serve as role models for young people. A recent poll conducted in secondary schools revealed that over 80 per cent of students wanted to be like their sporting heroes. These young people, the future of Australia, deserve better, don't they?

1 a Find an example of a rhetorical question in the above article.

____

____

b Provide an example of emotive language.

____

____

c Who is the expert referred to in the letter?

d What are the statistics that are referred to in the editorial and why do you think they have been used?

e Find an example of inclusive language in the letter.

2 Find examples of letters to the editor and discuss the persuasive techniques used by the writers.

3 Choose one of the following topics. You may decide to agree or disagree with the statement provided.

- School uniforms kill creativity.
- School canteens have a duty to keep Australia healthy.
- Boxing should be banned.

Write two letters to the editor on this topic. Choose your two types of letter from the following list:

- An angry letter
- A tactful letter
- A humorous letter
- A threatening letter
- An apologetically complaining letter

4 Write a letter to the editor about an issue in the news or in response to 'Lift Your Game, Fellas' or one of the following topics:

- Australian students do not do enough homework.
- Reality television is bad television.
- Pet shops should be banned.

Use at least one example of emotive language, one rhetorical question and one example of inclusive language in your letter. You should also refer to an expert and to one piece of statistical evidence. For the purpose of this exercise, these may be made up. Remember to set out your letter correctly.

WRITING UNIT 16 PROOFREADING FOR PARAGRAPHING AND PUNCTUATION

Before you submit your writing, you need to check it carefully to ensure that **punctuation** and **paragraphs** are correct. The many different types of writing in this book have different requirements in terms of paragraphs, although the use of punctuation is usually standard across all types of writing.

If you are in doubt about how to use punctuation and paragraphs, you could refer to a book such as *SkillWorks!* (OUP) to give you more detailed explanations and exercises.

It is a good idea to read your work aloud to check if the punctuation is correct. The end of a sentence usually requires a new breath (and a full stop), while a comma is used for smaller breaks. Do not forget to check for a capital letter after a full stop. If you are using dialogue (people's actual words to each other), check for opening and closing quotation marks (inverted commas) and do not forget to take a new line for each change of speaker.

1 Insert a question mark or a full stop at the end of the following sentences.

a Are you going to the movies tonight _____

b Wendy asked Tim if he was going to the pictures that night _____

c When will you ever learn _____

d I was going to ask my brother if he had a CD that I could borrow _____

e Why do you want to know _____

2 Rewrite the following sentences, including punctuation marks and capital letters where necessary.

a john this is my friend sam who will be helping us out today

____

____

b charlotte did not want blue purple or green socks

____

____

c well said mr smith with a laugh what are you waiting for

____

____

d daniel who was allergic to peanuts was careful to avoid them

____

____

e why are you running away asked the teacher

____

____

Not all types of writing require formal paragraphs. Below are some of the main types of writing covered in this book, with suggestions about the use of paragraphs.

When you are proofreading your work, check to see that it is set out appropriately.

Procedures or 'how to' guides can be written in paragraphs, but you may decide to use subheadings or dot points instead, especially if you are describing a practical procedure.

Reports, **résumés** and **job applications** are often written in sections with different subheadings, so the use of paragraphs will be different from narrative writing.

Summaries are obviously written briefly and paragraphs are not required.

Letters, **reviews**, **narratives**, **descriptions** and **expositions** are usually written in paragraphs.

You should start a new paragraph for the following reasons:

- Change of speaker. When you are writing dialogue, you should start a new line when someone else speaks.
- Change of time; for example, *the following morning* or *later that day*.
- Change of place. Start a new paragraph when you are writing about a different place.
- Change of person; for example, introducing another character.
- Change of ideas. Start a new paragraph when you introduce a new idea into your piece of writing.

3 The following sentences can be arranged into three small paragraphs. Paragraph 1 is an introductory paragraph, paragraph 2 indicates a change of place and paragraph 3 indicates a change of time. Indicate after each sentence whether it belongs to paragraph 1, 2 or 3.

a From the front lawn I could see flames engulfing the house. _____

b The next morning we surveyed the damage. _____

c I rushed out onto the front lawn. _____

d My mother woke me up in the middle of the night. _____

e I looked back at the house. _____

f We later discovered that the fire had been caused by an electrical fault. _____

g We had to stay at my grandmother's house for a while. _____

h I was sleeping peacefully. _____

i She told me to run out of the house immediately. _____

j I was really frightened. _____

4 You have been asked to write a review of a film you have seen recently. You will be allowed five paragraphs. What will be the main idea of each paragraph? Below is your plan. Briefly outline the content of each paragraph of your review.

Title of your review: ______________________________

Paragraph 1: ______________________________

Paragraph 2: ______________________________

Paragraph 3: ______________________________

Paragraph 4: ______________________________

Paragraph 5: ______________________________

WRITING UNIT 17 PROOFREADING FOR GRAMMAR: DOES IT MAKE SENSE?

There are a number of common mistakes that students make in relation to various rules of grammar, which can spoil their writing. These include:

- changing from one verb tense to another without a good reason
- writing in short sentences, which can make your writing seem jerky. Short sentences can be dramatic and strong, but you also need to be able to link several ideas together. You need to make use of conjunctions or joining words such as *although*, *if*, *since* to show the links between your ideas.
- using very long, wandering sentences that should be broken up into shorter ones. These last two dot points might seem contradictory but they are not. Skilful writers vary the length of their sentences because readers like variety.
- failing to add interesting detail to their writing by making full use of those very helpful adjectives, adjectival phrases and clauses, and verbs and adverbs. These allow you to add details that help the reader to imagine what you are describing more fully.
- not taking advantage of pronouns to make their writing more interesting and less repetitious

1 A student told his teacher that he wanted to write this personal piece in the present tense to make it seem as if it was happening now. He has made a couple of errors. Rewrite the passage so that he can see where he has gone wrong.

It is Christmas morning. I am so excited because my twin brother, Theo, and I reckon we are getting mountain bikes. I charge into his room and I woke him up. He chucked a pillow at me and we race down the stairs like idiots.

____

____

____

____

____

____

2 a Use the linking words provided to form one sentence from those listed below. Make any small changes necessary.

i Everyone respected the famous scientist.

The scientist had made many valuable contributions for the benefit of the human race. (*who*)

____

____

____

ii My little sister tried to convince me.

She had seen a ghost.

It carried its head under its arm. (*that*, *which*)

____

____

____

iii Our neighbour's husband died.

She decided to move.

She could start a new life. (*when, so that*)

____

____

b Join the following ideas together in any way you like. There are no clues provided. You can make small changes to the sentences if necessary.

i I had a hamburger for lunch.

The middle fell out.

It was cold.

____

____

ii I love going to the beach.

I hate getting sunburnt.

I always slather on the sunscreen.

____

____

iii I love reading books.

My brother prefers television.

We both like mysteries.

____

____

3 The following sentence is too long; break it up into two smaller sentences.
The dog next door barked all night and kept us all awake, so my father threw a shoe over the fence at him, but he still didn't shut up and we found out the next morning that he wrecked the shoe and we weren't very happy, but our neighbours didn't care.

____

____

____

____

____

____

____

____

____

____

NOTES

NOTES

FAMILY HISTORY WORKBOOK

In association with ancestry

YOUR **PRACTICAL GUIDE** FROM THE MAKERS OF Family Tree

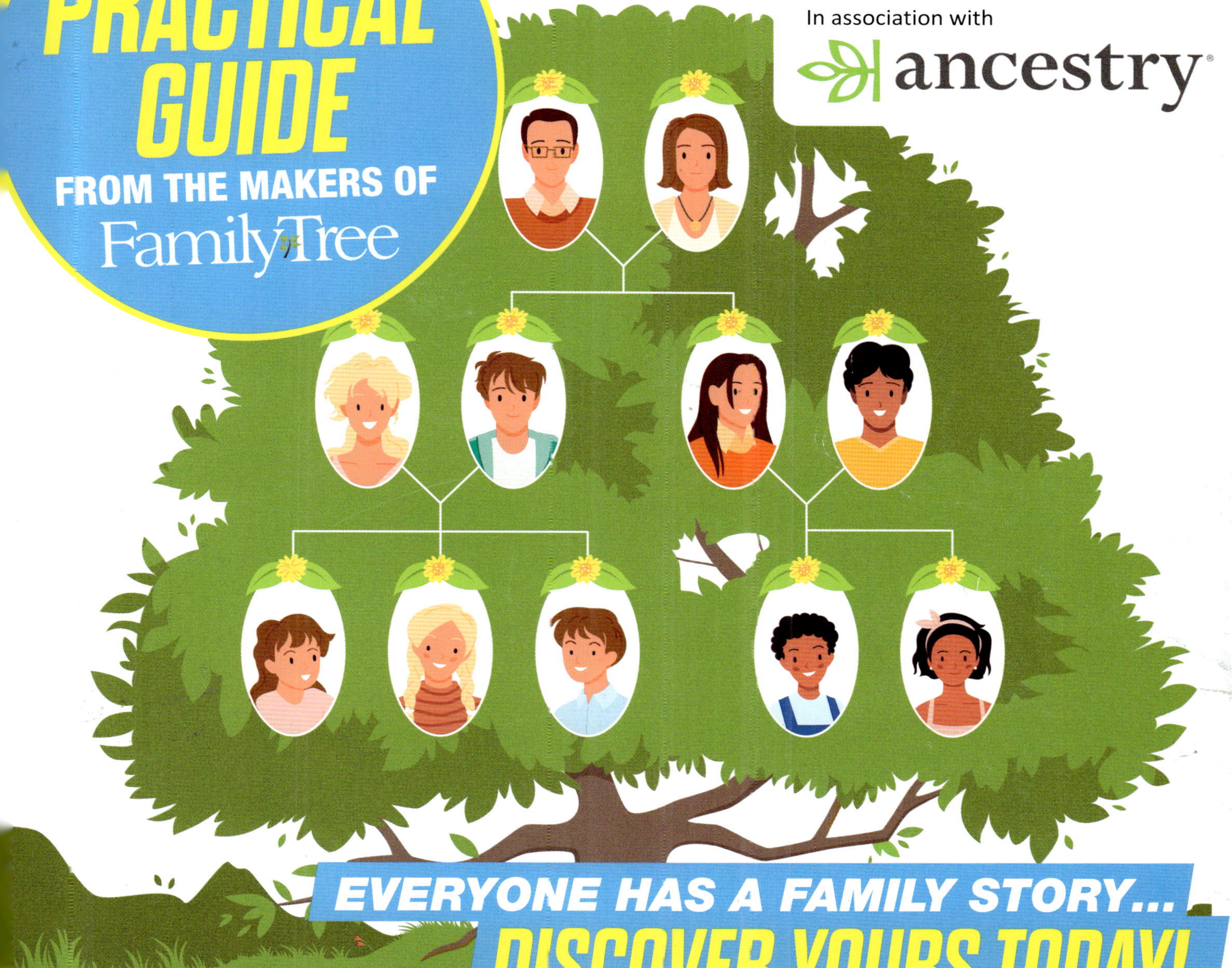

EVERYONE HAS A FAMILY STORY...

DISCOVER YOURS TODAY!

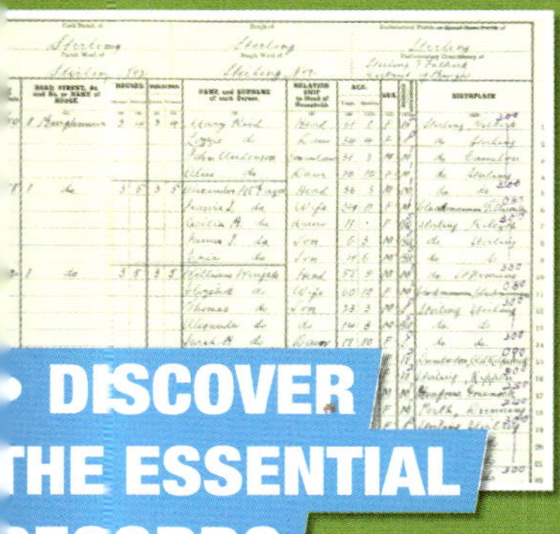

• DISCOVER THE ESSENTIAL RECORDS

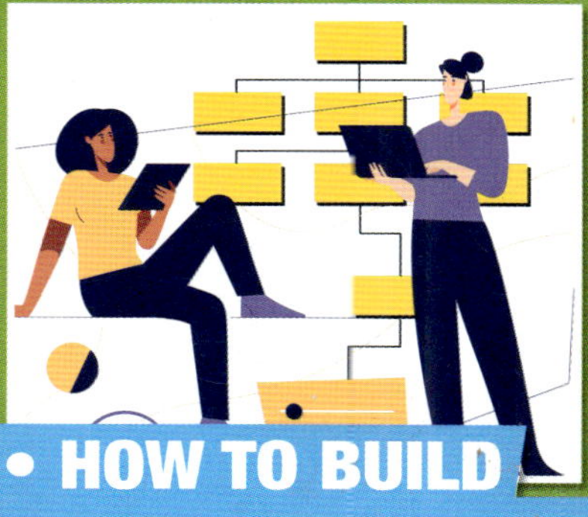

• HOW TO BUILD YOUR TREE ONLINE

• MASTER THE RESEARCH HACKS

WARNERS GROUP PUBLICATIONS

9 781910 525395 01

£11.99